Essential Series

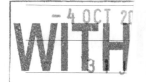

Spring

London
Berlin
Heidelberg
New York
Barcelona
Hong Kong
Milan
Paris
Singapore
Tokyo

Also in this series:

John Cowell
Essential Visual Basic 5.0 *fast*
3-540-76148-9

John Vince
Essential Computer Animation *fast*
1-85233-141-0

Duncan Reed and Peter Thomas
Essential HTML *fast*
3-540-76199-3

Aladdin Ayesh
Essential Dynamic HTML *fast*
1-85233-626-9

John Hunt
Essential JavaBeans *fast*
1-85233-032-5

David Thew
Essential Access 2000 *fast*
1-85233-295-6

John Vince
Essential Virtual Reality *fast*
1-85233-012-0

Ian Palmer
Essential Java 3D *fast*
1-85233-394-4

John Cowell
Essential Visual J++ 6.0 *fast*
1-85233-013-9

Matthew Norman
Essential ColdFusion *fast*
1-85233-315-4

John Cowell
Essential Java 2 *fast*
1-85233-071-6

Ian Chivers
Essential Linux *fast*
1-85233-408-8

John Cowell
Essential Visual Basic 6.0 *fast*
1-85233-071-6

Fiaz Hussain
Essential Flash 5.0 *fast*
1-85233-451-7

Ian Chivers
Essential Visual C++ 6.0 *fast*
1-85233-170-4

John Vince

Essential Mathematics for Computer Graphics *fast*

Springer

John Vince, MTech, PhD, FBCS, CEng
Media School, Bournemouth Univeristy,
Talbot Campus, Fern Barrow, Poole BH12 5BB, UK

Series Editor
John Cowell, BSc (Hons), MPhil, PhD
Department of Computer Science, De Montfort University, The Gateway,
Leicester LE1 9BH

British Library Cataloguing in Publication Data
Vince, John
   Essential mathematics for computer graphics fast. –
   (Essential series)
   1. Computer graphics – Mathematics
   I. Title II. Mathematics for computer graphics fast
   006.6'0151
   ISBN 1852333804

Library of Congress Cataloging-in-Publication Data
Vince, John (John A.)
   Essential mathematics for computer graphics fast / John Vince.
      p. cm. – (Essential series)
   Includes bibliographical references and index.
   ISBN 1-85233-380-4 (alk. paper)
   1. Computer graphics – Mathematics   I. Title.   II. Essential series (Springer-Verlag)

T385.V5614 2001
006.6'0151 – dc21   2001031424

ISBN 1-85233-380-4 Springer-Verlag London Berlin Heidelberg
a member of BertelsmannSpringer Science+Business Media GmbH
http://www.springer.co.uk

Typesetting: Mac Style, Scarborough
Printed and bound at The Cromwell Press, Trowbridge, Wiltshire
34/3830-543210 Printed on acid-free paper SPIN 10780791

Contents

1. MATHEMATICS **1**

Is mathematics difficult? 3

Who should read this book? 4

Aims and objectives of this book 4

Assumptions made in this book 5

How to use the book 5

2. NUMBERS **7**

Natural numbers 8

Prime numbers... 8

Integers 9

Rational numbers... 9

Irrational numbers 10

Real numbers 10

The number line 10

Complex numbers 10

Summary 13

3. ALGEBRA **15**

Notation 16

Algebraic laws.. 17

      Associative law 18

      Commutative law 18

      Distributive law 19

Solving the roots of a quadratic equation..................................... 19

Indices... 20

      Laws of indices 21

      Examples 21

Logarithms... 21

Further notation 23

Summary 23

4. TRIGONOMETRY **25**

The trigonometric ratios... 26

      Example.. 28

Inverse trigonometric ratios 28

Trigonometric relationships.. 29

The sine rule... 29

The cosine rule 30
Compound angles 30
Perimeter relationships 31
Summary 32

5.   CARTESIAN COORDINATES........................ 33
The Cartesian xy-plane 34
    Function graphs 36
    Geometric shapes 37
    Polygonal shapes 37
    Areas of shapes 38
    Theorem of Pythagoras in 2D 39
3D coordinates 40
    Theorem of Pythagoras in 3D 40
    3D polygons 41
    Euler's rule 41
Summary 42

6.   VECTORS 43
2D vectors 45
    Vector notation 45
    Graphical representation of vectors 45
    Magnitude of a vector 47
3D vectors 49
    Vector manipulation 49
    Multiplying a vector by a scalar 50
    Vector addition and subtraction 50
    Position vectors 51
    Unit vectors 52
    Cartesian vectors 53
    Vector multiplication 54
    Scalar product 55
    Example of the dot product 57
    The dot product in lighting calculations 58
    The dot product in back-face detection 59
    The vector product 60
    The right-hand rule 64
Deriving a unit normal vector for a triangle 65
Areas 66
    Calculating 2D areas 67
Summary 68

Contents

7. TRANSFORMATIONS 69

2D transformations	70
Translation	70
Scaling	70
Reflection	71
Matrices	72
Systems of notation	75
The determinant of a matrix	76
Homogeneous coordinates	77
2D translation	79
2D scaling	79
2D reflections	80
2D shearing	82
2D rotation	83
2D scaling	86
2D reflections	87
2D rotation about an arbitrary point	88
3D transformations	89
3D translation	89
3D scaling	90
3D rotations	90
Gimbal lock	95
Rotating about an axis	96
3D reflections	98
Change of axes	98
2D change of axes	99
Direction cosines	100
Positioning the virtual camera	102
Direction cosines	103
Euler angles	106
Quaternions	110
Adding and subtracting quaternions	110
Multiplying quaternions	111
The inverse quaternion	111
Rotating points about an axis	112
Roll, pitch and yaw quaternions	116
Quaternions in matrix form	118
Frames of reference	119
Transforming vectors	120
Determinants	122
Perspective projection	126
Summary	128

8.   INTERPOLATION **129**
Linear interpolant 130
Non-linear interpolation 133
    Trigonometric interpolation.. 133
    Cubic interpolation 135
Interpolating vectors 141
Interpolating quaternions 145
Summary 147

9.   CURVES AND PATCHES **149**
The circle 150
The ellipse 151
Bézier curves 152
    Bernstein polynomials 152
    Quadratic Bézier curves 157
    Cubic Bernstein polynomials... 158
A recursive Bézier formula... 162
Bézier curves using matrices 162
    Linear interpolation 164
B-splines 167
    Uniform B-splines 168
    Continuity 171
    Non-uniform B-splines 172
    Non-uniform Rational B-Splines 172
Surface patches 173
    Planar surface patch 173
    Quadratic Bézier surface patch 174
    Cubic Bézier surface patch 177
Summary 180

10. ANALYTIC GEOMETRY **181**
Review of geometry.. 182
    Angles 182
    Intercept theorems 183
    Golden Section 184
    Triangles 185
    Center of gravity of a triangle 185
    Isosceles triangle 186
    Equilateral triangle 187
    Right triangle 187
    Theorem of Thales 187
    Theorem of Pythagoras 188
    Quadrilateral.. 188

Contents

Trapezoid 189
Parallelogram 189
Rhombus 190
Regular polygon (n-gon) 190
Circle 192
2D analytic geometry 193
Equation of a straight line 193
The Hessian normal form 194
Space partitioning 197
The Hessian normal form from two points 198
Intersection points 199
Intersection point of two straight lines 199
Intersection point of two line segments 199
Point inside a triangle 202
Area of a triangle 202
Hessian normal form 205
Intersection of a circle with a straight line 207
3D geometry 209
Equation of a straight line 209
Point of intersection of two straight lines 211
Equation of a plane 215
Space partitioning 216
Point of intersection of a line and a plane 216
Point of intersection of a line segment and a plane 218
Summary 219

11. CONCLUSION 221

REFERENCES 223

INDEX 225

Chapter

1

Mathematics

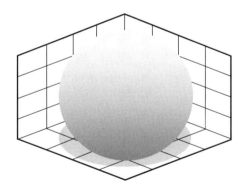

When I was taught mathematics at junior school in the late 1950s, there were no computers or calculators. Calculations, whether they were addition, subtraction, multiplication, division or square roots, had to be worked out in one's head or with pencil and paper. We learnt our 'times tables' by reciting them over and over again until we could give the product of any pair of numbers up to 12 – numbers higher than 12 were computed long hand.

I was fortunate in having a teacher who appreciated the importance of mathematics, and without knowing it at the time, I began a journey into a subject area that would eventually bring my knowledge of mathematics to life in computer graphics.

Today, students have access to calculators that are virtually miniature computers. They are programmable and can even display graphs on small LCD screens. Unfortunately, the policy pursued by some schools has ensured that generations of children are unable to compute simple arithmetic operations without the aid of a calculator. I believe that such children have been disadvantaged, as they are unable to visualize the various patterns that exist in numbers such as odd numbers $(1, 3, 5, 7, \ldots)$, even numbers $(2, 4, 6, 8, \ldots)$, prime numbers $(2, 3, 5, 7, 11, \ldots)$, squares $(1, 4, 9, 16, 25, \ldots)$ and Fibonacci numbers $(0, 1, 1, 2, 3, 5, 8, \ldots)$. They will not know that it is possible to multiply a two-digit number, such as 17, by 11, simply by adding 1 to 7 and placing the result in the middle to make 187.

Although I do appreciate the benefits of calculators, I believe that they are introduced into the curriculum far too early. Children should be given the opportunity to develop a sense of number, and the possibility of developing a love for mathematics, before they discover the tempting features of a digital calculator.

'I am no good at mathematics' is a common response from most people when asked about their mathematical abilities. Some suggest that their brain is unable to cope with numbers, some claim that it's boring, and others put it down to inadequate teaching. Personally, I am not very good at mathematics, but I delight in reading books about mathematicians and the history of mathematics, and applying mathematics to solve problems in computer graphics. I am easily baffled by pages of abstract mathematical symbols, but readily understand the application of mathematics in a practical context.

It was only when I started programming computers to produce drawings and pictures that I really appreciated the usefulness of mathematics. Multiplication became synonymous with scaling; division created perspective; sines and cosines rotated objects; tangents produced shearing, and geometry and trigonometry provided the analytical tools to solve all sorts of other problems. Such a toolkit is readily understood and remembered.

Is mathematics difficult?

'Is mathematics difficult?' I suppose that there is no real answer to this question, because it all depends upon what we mean by 'mathematics' and 'difficult'. But if the question is rephrased slightly: 'Is the mathematics of computer graphics difficult?' then the answer is a definite no. What's more, I believe that the subject of computer graphics can instill in someone a love for mathematics. Perhaps 'love' is too strong a word, but I am convinced that it is possible to 'make friends' with mathematics.

For me, mathematics should be treated like a foreign language: You only need to learn an appropriate vocabulary to survive while visiting another country. If you attempt to memorize an extended vocabulary, and do not put it into practice, it is highly likely that you will forget it. Mathematics is the same. I know that if I attempted to memorize some obscure branch of mathematics, such as vector calculus, I would forget it within days if I did not put it to some practical use.

Fortunately, the mathematics needed for computer graphics is reasonably simple and covers only a few branches such as algebra, trigonometry, vectors, geometry, transforms, interpolation, curves and patches. Although these topics do have an advanced side to them, in most applications we only need to explore their intermediate levels.

Who should read this book?

I have written this book as a reference for anyone intending to study topics such as computer graphics, computer animation, computer games or virtual reality, especially for people who want to understand the technical aspects. Although it is possible to study these topics without requiring the support of mathematics, increasingly, there are situations and projects that require animators, programmers and technical directors to resort to mathematics to resolve unforeseen technical problems. This may be in the form of a script or an extra piece of program code.

Aims and objectives of this book

One of the aims of this book is to bring together a range of useful mathematical topics that are relevant to computer graphics. And the real objective is to provide programmers and animators with an understanding of mathematics so that they can solve all sorts of problems with confidence.

I have attempted to do this by exploring a range of mathematical topics, without intimidating the reader with mathematical symbols and abstract ideas. Hopefully, I will be able to explain each topic in a simple and practical manner, with a variety of practical examples.

This is far from being an exhaustive study of the mathematics associated with computer graphics. Each chapter introduces the reader to a new topic, and should leave the reader confident and capable of studying more advanced books.

Assumptions made in this book

I suppose that I do expect that readers will have some understanding of arithmetic and a general knowledge of the principles of mathematics, such as the ideas of algebra. But, apart from that, each subject will be introduced as though it were the first time it had been discovered.

In the chapter on curves and surfaces I have used a little calculus. Readers who have not studied this subject should not be concerned about missing some vital piece of information. I only included it to keep the explanation complete.

How to use the book

I would advise starting at the beginning and proceeding chapter by chapter. Where a subject seems familiar, just jump ahead until a challenge is discovered. Once you have read the book, keep it handy so that you can refer to it when the occasion arises.

Although I have tried to maintain a sequence to the mathematical ideas, so that one idea leads to another, in some cases this has proved impossible. For example, determinants are referred to in the chapter on vectors, but they are described in detail in the next chapter on transforms. Similarly, the later chapter on analytic geometry contains some basic ideas of geometry, but its position was dictated by its use of vectors. Consequently, on some occasions, the reader will have to move between chapters to read about related topics.

Chapter

2

Numbers

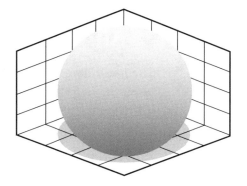

All sorts of number systems have been proposed by previous civilizations, but our current system is a positional number system using a base 10. The number 1234 really means the sum of one thousand, plus two hundreds, plus three tens, plus four ones, which can be expressed as $1 \times 1000 + 2 \times 100 + 3 \times 10 + 4 \times 1$. It should be obvious that the base 10 is nothing special, it just so happens that human beings have evolved with 10 digits, which we use for counting. This suggests that any number can be used as a base: 2, 3, 4, 5, 6, 7, etc. In fact, the decimal number system is not very convenient for computer technology, where electronic circuits switch on and off billions of times a second using binary numbers – numbers to a base 2 – with great ease. In this text there is no real need to explore such numbers. This can be left to programmers who have to master number systems such as binary (base 2), octal (base 8) and hexadecimal (base 16).

The only features of numbers we have to revise in this chapter are the families of numbers that exist, what they are used for, and any problems that arise when they are stored in a computer. Let's begin with the natural numbers.

Natural numbers

The *natural numbers* $\{0, 1, 2, 3, 4, \ldots\}$ are used for counting, ordering and labelling. Note that negative numbers are not included. We often use natural numbers to subscript a quantity to distinguish one element from another, e.g. $x_1, x_2, x_3, x_4, \ldots$.

Prime numbers

A natural number that can be divided only by 1 and itself, without leaving a remainder, is called a *prime number*. Examples are $\{2, 3, 5, 7, 11, 13, 17\}$. There are 25 primes less than 100, 168 primes less than 1000 and 455 052 512 primes less than 10 000 000 000. The *fundamental theory of arithmetic* states, 'Any positive integer (other than 1) can be written as the product of prime numbers in one and only one way.' For example, $25 = 5 \times 5$; $26 = 2 \times 13$; $27 = 3 \times 3 \times 3$; $28 = 2 \times 2 \times 7$; $29 = 29$; $30 = 2 \times 3 \times 5$ and $92\,365 = 5 \times 7 \times 7 \times 13 \times 29$.

In 1742 Christian Goldbach conjectured that every even integer greater than 2 could be written as the sum of two primes:

$4 = 2 + 2$
$14 = 11 + 3$
$18 = 11 + 7$, etc.

No one has ever found an exception to this conjecture, and no one has ever proved it.

Although prime numbers are enigmatic and have taxed the brains of the greatest mathematicians, unfortunately they play no part in computer graphics!

Integers

Integers include negative numbers, as follows: $\{\ldots -3, -2, -1, 0, 1, 2, 3, 4, \ldots\}$.

Rational numbers

Rational or *fractional* numbers are numbers that can be represented as a fraction. For example, 2, $\sqrt{16}$, 0.25 are rational numbers because

$$2 = \frac{4}{2}, \quad \sqrt{16} = 4 = \frac{8}{2}, \quad 0.25 = \frac{1}{4}$$

Some rational numbers can be stored accurately inside a computer, but many others can only be stored approximately. For example, $4/3 = 1.333\,333\ldots$ produces an infinite sequence of threes and has to be truncated when stored as a binary number.

Irrational numbers

Irrational numbers cannot be represented as fractions. Examples are $\sqrt{2} = 1.414\,213\,562\ldots$, $\pi = 3.141\,592\,65\ldots$ and $e = 2.718\,281\,828\ldots$ Such numbers never terminate and are always subject to a small error when stored within a computer.

Real numbers

Rational and irrational numbers together comprise the *real numbers*.

The number line

It is convenient to organize numbers in the form of an axis to give them a spatial significance. Figure 2.1 shows such a *number line*, which forms an axis as used in graphs and coordinate systems. The number line also helps us understand complex numbers, which are the 'king' of all numbers.

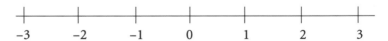

Figure 2.1 *The number line.*

Complex numbers

Leonhard Euler (1707–1783) (whose name rhymes with *boiler*) played a significant role in putting *complex numbers* on the map. His ideas on rotations are also used in computer graphics to locate objects and virtual cameras in space, as we shall see later on.

Complex numbers resolve some awkward problems that arise when we attempt to solve certain types of equations. For example, $x^2 - 4 = 0$ has solutions $x = \pm 2$. But $x^2 + 4 = 0$ has no obvious solutions using real or integer numbers. However, the number line provides a graphical interpretation for a new type of number, the complex number. The name is rather misleading: it is not complex, it is rather simple.

Consider the scenario depicted in Figure 2.2. Any number on the number line is related to the same number with the opposite sign via an anti-clockwise rotation of 180°. For example, if 3 is rotated 180° about zero it becomes -3, and if -2 is rotated 180° about zero it becomes 2.

We can now write $-3 = (-1) \times 3$, or $2 = (-1) \times -2$, where -1 is effectively a rotation through 180°. But a rotation of 180° can be interpreted as two consecutive rotations of 90°, and the question now arises: What does a rotation of 90° signify? Well, let's assume that we don't know what the answer is going to be – even though some of you do – we can at least give a name to the operation, and what better name to use than i.

So the letter i represents an anticlockwise rotation of 90°. Therefore i2 is equivalent to lifting 2 out of the number line, rotating it 90° and leaving it hanging in limbo. But if we take this 'imaginary' number and subject it to a further 90° rotation, i.e. ii2, it becomes -2. Therefore, we can write ii2 = -2, which means that ii = -1. But if this is so, i = $\sqrt{-1}$!

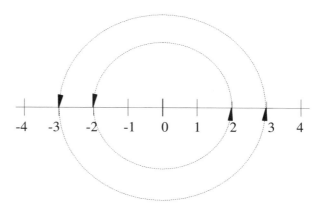

Figure 2.2 *Rotating numbers through 180° reverses their sign.*

This gives rise to two types of number: real numbers and complex numbers. Real numbers are the everyday numbers we use for counting and so on, whereas complex numbers have a mixture of real and imaginary components, and help resolve a wide range of mathematical problems.

Figure 2.3 shows how complex numbers are represented: the horizontal number line represents the *real component*, and the vertical number line represents the *imaginary component*.

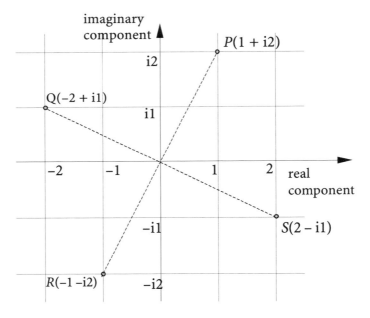

Figure 2.3 *The graphical representation of complex numbers.*

For example, the complex number $P(1 + i2)$ in Figure 2.3 can be rotated 90° to Q by multiplying it by i. However, we must remember that $ii = -1$:

$$i(1 + i2) \quad = i1 + ii2$$
$$= i1 - 2$$
$$= -2 + i1$$

$Q(-2 + i1)$ can be rotated another 90° to R by multiplying it by i:

$$i(-2 + i1) = i(-2) + ii1$$
$$= -i2 - 1$$
$$= -1 - i2$$

$R(-1 - i2)$ in turn, can be rotated 90° to S by multiplying it by i:

$$i(-1 - i2) = i(-1) - ii2$$
$$= -i1 + 2$$
$$= 2 - i1$$

Finally, $S(2 - i1)$ can be rotated 90° to P by multiplying it by i:

$$i(2 - i1) = i2 - ii1$$
$$= i2 + 1$$
$$= 1 + i2$$

Although we rarely use complex numbers in computer graphics, we can see that they are intimately related to Cartesian coordinates, and that the ordered pair $(x, y) \equiv x + iy$.

Before concluding this chapter, I cannot fail to include the famous equation discovered by Euler:

$$e^{i\pi} + 1 = 0 \qquad\qquad (2.1)$$

which integrates 0, 1, e, π and i in a simple and beautiful arrangement, and is on a par with Einstein's $e = mc^2$.

Summary

This short chapter made sure that the terminology of numbers was understood, and now provides a good link into the basics of algebra.

Chapter 3

Algebra

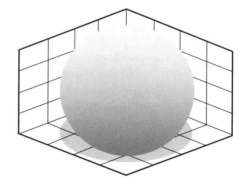

This chapter reviews the basic elements of algebra to prepare the reader for the algebraic manipulations used in later chapters. Although algebra can be a very abstract mathematical tool, here we only need to explore those practical features relevant to its application to computer graphics.

Notation

The word *'algebra'* comes from the Arabic *al-jabr w'al-muqabal*, meaning 'restoration and reduction'. Today's algebraic notation has evolved over thousands of years during which different civilizations have developed ways of annotating mathematical and logical problems. In retrospect, it does seem strange that centuries passed before the 'equals' sign (=) was invented and concepts such as 'zero' (CE 876) were introduced, especially as they now seem so important. But we are not at the end of this evolution, because new forms of annotation and manipulation will continue to emerge as new mathematical ideas are invented.

One fundamental concept of algebra is the idea of giving a name to an unknown quantity. For example, m is often used to represent the slope of a 2D line, and c is the line's *y-coordinate* where it intersects the y-axis. René Descartes (1596–1650) formalized the idea of using letters from the beginning of the alphabet (a, b, c, etc.) to represent arbitrary numbers, and letters at the end of the alphabet ($p, q, r, s, t, \ldots x, y, z$) to identify variables representing quantities such as pressure (p), temperature (t), and coordinates (x, y, z).

With the aid of the basic arithmetic operators $+, -, \times, \div$ we can develop expressions that describe the behaviour of a physical process or a specific computation. For example, the expression $ax + by - d$ equals zero for a straight line. The variables x and y are the coordinates of any point on the line and the values of a, b, d determine the position and orientation of the line. There is an implied multiplication between ax and by, which would be expressed as $a*x$ and $b*y$ if we were using a programming language.

The = sign permits the line equation to be expressed as a self-evident statement: $0 = ax + by - d$. Such a statement implies that the expressions on the left- and right-hand sides of the = sign are 'equal' or 'balanced'. So whatever is done to one side must also be done to the other in order to maintain equality or balance. For example, if we add d to both sides, the straight-line equation becomes $d = ax + by$. Similarly, we could double or treble both expressions, divide them by 4, or add 6, without disturbing the underlying relationship.

Algebraic expressions also contain a wide variety of other notation, such as

$\sqrt{x}$ square root of x

$\sqrt[n]{x}$ nth root of x

x^n x to the power n

$\sin(x)$ sine of x

$\cos(x)$ cosine of x

$\tan(x)$ tangent of x

$\log(x)$ logarithm of x

$\ln(x)$ natural logarithm of x

Parentheses are used to isolate part of an expression in order to select a sub-expression that is manipulated in a particular way. For example, the parentheses in $c(a + b) + d$ ensure that the variables a and b are added together before being multiplied by c and finally added to d.

Algebraic laws

There are three basic laws that are fundamental to manipulating algebraic expressions: associative, commutative and distributive. In the following descriptions, the term *binary operation* represents the arithmetic operations +, − or ×, which are always associated with a pair of numbers or variables.

Associative law

The *associative law* in algebra states that when three or more elements are linked together through a binary operation, the result is independent of how each pair of elements is grouped. The associative law of addition is

$$a + (b + c) = (a + b) + c \qquad (3.1)$$

e.g. $1 + (2 + 3) = (1 + 2) + 3$

and the associative law of multiplication is

$$a \times (b \times c) = (a \times b) \times c \qquad (3.2)$$

e.g. $1 \times (2 \times 3) = (1 \times 2) \times 3$

Note that subtraction is not associative:

$$a - (b - c) \neq (a - b) - c \qquad (3.3)$$

e.g. $1 - (2 - 3) \neq (1 - 2) - 3$

Commutative law

The *commutative law* in algebra states that when two elements are linked through some binary operation, the result is independent of the order of the elements. The commutative law of addition is

$$a + b = b + a \qquad (3.4)$$

e.g. $1 + 2 = 2 + 1$

and the commutative law of multiplication is

$$a \times b = b \times a \qquad (3.5)$$

e.g. $2 \times 3 = 3 \times 2$

Note that subtraction is not commutative:

$$a - b \neq b - a \qquad (3.6)$$

e.g. $2 - 3 \neq 3 - 2$

Distributive law

The *distributive law* in algebra describes an operation which when performed on a combination of elements is the same as performing the operation on the individual elements. The distributive law does not work in all cases of arithmetic. For example, multiplication over addition holds:

$$a \times (b + c) = ab + ac \tag{3.7}$$

e.g. $3 \times (4 + 5) = 3 \times 4 + 3 \times 5$

whereas addition over multiplication does not:

$$a + (b \times c) \neq (a + b) \times (a + c) \tag{3.8}$$

e.g. $3 + (4 \times 5) \neq (3 + 4) \times (3 + 5)$

Although most of these laws seem to be natural for numbers, they do not necessarily apply to all mathematical constructs. For instance, the *vector product*, which multiplies two vectors together, is not commutative.

Solving the roots of a quadratic equation

To put the above laws and notation into practice, let's take a simple example to illustrate the logical steps in solving a problem. The task involves solving the roots of a quadratic equation, i.e. those values of x that make the equation equal zero.

Given the quadratic equation where $a \neq 0$:

$$ax^2 + bx + c = 0$$

Step 1: subtract c from both sides:

$$ax^2 + bx = -c$$

Step 2: divide both sides by a:

$$x^2 + \frac{b}{a}x = -\frac{c}{a}$$

Step 3: add $\dfrac{b^2}{4a^2}$ to both sides:

$$x^2 + \frac{b}{a}x + \frac{b^2}{4a^2} = -\frac{c}{a} + \frac{b^2}{4a^2}$$

Step 4: factorize the left side:

$$\left(x + \frac{b}{2a}\right)^2 = -\frac{c}{a} + \frac{b^2}{4a^2}$$

Step 5: make $4a^2$ the common denominator for the right side:

$$\left(x + \frac{b}{2a}\right)^2 = \frac{-4ac + b^2}{4a^2}$$

Step 6: take the square root of both sides:

$$x + \frac{b}{2a} = \frac{\pm\sqrt{b^2 - 4ac}}{2a}$$

Step 7: subtract $\dfrac{b}{2a}$ from both sides:

$$x = \frac{\pm\sqrt{b^2 - 4ac}}{2a} - \frac{b}{2a}$$

Step 8: rearrange the right side:

$$x = \frac{-b \pm \sqrt{b^2 - 4ac}}{2a} \tag{3.9}$$

This last expression gives the roots for any quadratic equation.

Indices

A notation for repeated multiplication is with the use of indices. For instance, in the above example with a quadratic equation x^2 is used to represent $x \times x$. This notation leads to a variety of situations where laws are required to explain how the result is to be computed.

Laws of indices

The laws of indices can be expressed as

$$a^m \times a^n = a^{m+n} \tag{3.10}$$

$$a^m \div a^n = a^{m-n} \tag{3.11}$$

$$\left(a^m\right)^n = a^{mn} \tag{3.12}$$

which are easily verified using some simple examples.

Examples

1: $2^3 \times 2^2 = 8 \times 4 = 32 = 2^5$

2: $2^4 \div 2^2 = 16 \div 4 = 4 = 2^2$

3: $(2^2)^3 = 64 = 2^6$

From the above laws, it is evident that

$$a^0 = 1 \tag{3.13}$$

$$a^{-p} = \frac{1}{a^p} \tag{3.14}$$

$$a^{\frac{p}{q}} = \sqrt[q]{a^p} \tag{3.15}$$

Logarithms

Two people are associated with the invention of logarithms: John Napier (1550–1617) and Joost Bürgi (1552–1632). Both men were frustrated by the time they spent multiplying numbers together, and both realized that multiplication could be replaced by addition using logarithms. Logarithms exploit the addition and subtraction of indices shown in (3.10) and (3.11), and are always associated with a base. For example, if $a^x = n$, then $\log_a n = x$, where a is the base. A concrete example brings the idea to life:

if $10^2 = 100$ then $\log_{10} 100 = 2$

which can be interpreted as '10 has to be raised to the power (index) 2 to equal 100'. The log operation finds the power of the base for a given number.

Thus a multiplication can be translated into an addition using logs:

$36 \times 24 = 864$

$\log_{10} 36 + \log_{10} 24 = \log_{10} 864$

$1.55630250077 + 1.38021124171 = 2.93651374248$

In general, the two bases used in calculators and computer software are 10 and 2.718281846.... The latter is e, a *transcendental* number. (A transcendental number is not a root of any algebraic equation. Joseph Liouville proved the existence of such numbers in 1844. π, the ratio of the circumference of a circle to its diameter, is another example.) To distinguish one type of logarithm from the other, logarithms to the base 10 are written as log, and logarithms to the base e are written as ln.

From the above notation, it is evident that

$$\log (ab) = \log a + \log b \qquad (3.16)$$

$$\log\left(\frac{a}{b}\right) = \log a - \log b \qquad (3.17)$$

$$\log\left(a^n\right) = n \log a \qquad (3.18)$$

$$\log\left(\sqrt[n]{a}\right) = \frac{1}{n} \log a \qquad (3.19)$$

The following formula is useful to convert from the base 10 to the base e:

$$\log a = \ln a \times \log e = 0.4343 \ln a \qquad (3.20)$$

Further notation

Mathematicians use all sorts of symbols to substitute for natural language expressions. Here are some examples:

< less than

> greater than

≤ less than or equal to

≥ greater than or equal to

≅ approximately equal to

≡ equivalent to

≠ not equal to

For example, $0 \le t \le 1$ can be interpreted as: 0 is less than or equal to t, which is less than or equal to 1. Basically, this means t varies between 0 and 1.

Summary

The above description of algebra should be sufficient for the reader to understand the remaining chapters. However, one should remember that this is only the beginning of a very complex subject.

Chapter
4

Trigonometry

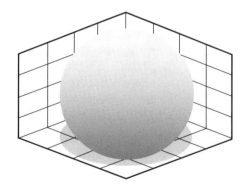

When we split the word 'trigonometry' into its constituent parts, *'tri'* *'gon'* *'metry'*, we see that it is to do with the measurement of three-sided polygons, i.e. triangles. It is a very ancient subject, and one the reader requires to understand for the analysis and solution of problems in computer graphics.

Trigonometric functions arise in vectors, transforms, geometry, quaternions and interpolation, and in this chapter we will survey some of the basic features with which the reader should be familiar.

The measurement of angles is at the heart of trigonometry, and two units of angular measurement have survived into modern usage: *degrees* and *radians*. The degree (or sexagesimal) unit of measure derives from defining one complete rotation as 360°. Each degree divides into 60 minutes, and each minute divides into 60 seconds. The number 60 has survived from Mesopotamian days and is rather incongruous when used alongside today's decimal system – which is why the radian has secured a strong foothold in modern mathematics.

The radian of angular measure does not depend on any arbitrary constant. It is the angle created by a circular arc whose length is equal to the circle's radius. And because the perimeter of a circle is $2\pi r$, 2π radians correspond to one complete rotation. As 360° correspond to 2π radians, 1 radian corresponds to $180/\pi°$, which is approximately 57.3°.

The reader should try to memorize the following relationships between radians and degrees:

$$\frac{\pi}{2} = 90°, \quad \pi = 180°, \quad \frac{3\pi}{2} = 270°, \quad 2\pi = 360°$$

The trigonometric ratios

Ancient civilizations knew that triangles, whatever their size, possessed some inherent properties, especially the ratios of sides and their associated angles. This meant that if such ratios were known in advance, problems involving triangles with unknown lengths and angles could be computed using these ratios.

To give you some idea why we employ the current notation, consider the history of the word sine. The Hindu word *ardha-jya* meaning 'half-chord' was abbreviated to *jya* ('chord'), which was translated by the Arabs into *jiba*, and corrupted to *jb*. Other translators converted this to *jaib*, meaning 'cove', 'bulge' or 'bay', which in Latin is *sinus*.

Today, the trigonometric ratios are commonly known by the abbreviations sin, cos, tan, cosec, sec and cot. Figure 4.1 shows a right-angled triangle where the trigonometric ratios are given by

$$\sin(\beta) = \frac{opposite}{hypotenuse} \quad \cos(\beta) = \frac{adjacent}{hypotenuse} \quad \tan(\beta) = \frac{opposite}{adjacent}$$

$$\operatorname{cosec}(\beta) = \frac{1}{\sin(\beta)} \quad \sec(\beta) = \frac{1}{\cos(\beta)} \quad \cot(\beta) = \frac{1}{\tan(\beta)}$$

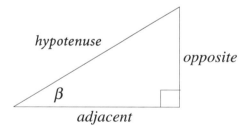

Figure 4.1 *Labeling a right-angle triangle for the trigonometric ratios.*

The sin and cos functions have limits ±1, whereas tan has limits ±∞. The signs of the functions in the four quadrants are

+	+	−	+	−	+
−	−	−	+	+	−

sin   cos   tan

Example

Figure 4.2 shows a triangle where the hypotenuse and one angle are known. The other sides are calculated as follows:

$$\frac{h}{10} = \sin(50°)$$

$$h = 10 \sin(50°) = 10 \times 0.76601$$

$$h = 7.66$$

$$\frac{b}{10} = \cos(50°)$$

$$b = 10 \cos(50°) = 10 \times 0.64279$$

$$b = 6.4279$$

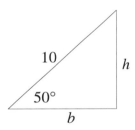

Figure 4.2 *h and b are unknown.*

Inverse trigonometric ratios

As every angle has its associated ratio, functions are required to convert one into the other. The sin, cos and tan functions convert angles into ratios, and the inverse functions $\sin^{-1}$, $\cos^{-1}$ and $\tan^{-1}$ convert ratios into angles. For example, $\sin(45°) = 0.707$, therefore $\sin^{-1}(0.707) = 45°$. Although the sin and cos functions are *cyclic* functions (i.e. they repeat indefinitely) the inverse functions return angles over a specific period.

Trigonometric relationships

There is an intimate relationship between the sin and cos definitions, and the are formally related by

$$\cos(\beta) = \sin(\beta + 90°)$$

Also, the theorem of Pythagoras can be used to derive other formulae such as

$$\frac{\sin(\beta)}{\cos(\beta)} = \tan(\beta)$$

$$\sin^2(\beta) + \cos^2(\beta) = 1$$

$$1 + \tan^2(\beta) = \sec^2(\beta)$$

$$1 + \cot^2(\beta) = \csc^2(\beta)$$

The sine rule

The sine rule relates angles and side lengths for a triangle. Figure 4.3 shows a triangle labelled such that side a is opposite angle A, side b is opposite angle B, etc.

The sine rule states

$$\frac{a}{\sin A} = \frac{b}{\sin B} = \frac{c}{\sin C}$$

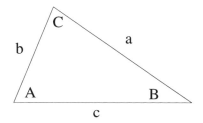

Figure 4.3 An arbitrary triangle.

The cosine rule

The cosine rule expresses the $\sin^2(\beta) + \cos^2(\beta) = 1$ relationship for the arbitrary triangle shown in Figure 4.3. In fact, there are three versions:

$$a^2 = b^2 + c^2 - 2bc\cos(A)$$

$$b^2 = c^2 + a^2 - 2ca\cos(B)$$

$$c^2 = a^2 + b^2 - 2ab\cos(C)$$

Three further relationships also hold:

$$a = b\cos(C) + c\cos(B)$$

$$b = c\cos(A) + a\cos(C)$$

$$c = a\cos(B) + b\cos(A)$$

Compound angles

Two sets of compound trigonometric relationships show how to add and subtract two different angles and multiples of the same angle. The following are some of the most common relationships:

$$\sin(A \pm B) = \sin(A)\cos(B) \pm \cos(A)\sin(B)$$

$$\cos(A \pm B) = \cos(A)\cos(B) \mp \sin(A)\sin(B)$$

$$\tan(A \pm B) = \frac{\tan(A) \pm \tan(B)}{1 \mp \tan(A)\tan(B)}$$

$$\sin(2\beta) = 2\sin(\beta)\cos(\beta)$$

$$\cos(2\beta) = \cos^2(\beta) - \sin^2(\beta)$$

$$\cos(2\beta) = 2\cos^2(\beta) - 1$$

$$\cos(2\beta) = 1 - 2\sin^2(\beta)$$

$$\sin(3\beta) = 3\sin(\beta) - 4\sin^3(\beta)$$

$$\cos(3\beta) = 4\cos^3(\beta) - 3\cos(\beta)$$

$$\cos^2(\beta) = \tfrac{1}{2}\left(1 + \cos(2\beta)\right)$$

$$\sin^2(\beta) = \tfrac{1}{2}\left(1 - \cos(2\beta)\right)$$

Perimeter relationships

Finally, referring back to Figure 4.3, we come to the relationships that integrate angles with the perimeter of a triangle:

$$s = \frac{1}{2}(a + b + c)$$

$$\sin\left(\frac{A}{2}\right) = \sqrt{\frac{(s-b)(s-c)}{bc}}$$

$$\sin\left(\frac{B}{2}\right) = \sqrt{\frac{(s-c)(s-a)}{ca}}$$

$$\sin\left(\frac{C}{2}\right) = \sqrt{\frac{(s-a)(s-b)}{ab}}$$

$$\cos\left(\frac{A}{2}\right) = \sqrt{\frac{s(s-a)}{bc}}$$

$$\cos\left(\frac{B}{2}\right) = \sqrt{\frac{s(s-b)}{ca}}$$

$$\cos\left(\frac{C}{2}\right) = \sqrt{\frac{s(s-c)}{ab}}$$

$$\sin(A) = \frac{2}{bc}\sqrt{s(s-a)(s-b)(s-c)}$$

$$\sin(B) = \frac{2}{ca}\sqrt{s(s-a)(s-b)(s-c)}$$

$$\sin(C) = \frac{2}{ab}\sqrt{s(s-a)(s-b)(s-c)}$$

Summary

No derivation has been given for the formulae in this chapter, but the reader who is really interested will find plenty of books that show their origins. Hopefully, the formulae will be a useful reference when studying the rest of the book, and perhaps will be of some use when solving problems in the future.

I should draw the reader's attention to two maths books that I have found a source of information and inspiration: *Handbook of Mathematics and Computational Science* by John Harris and Horst Stocker (1998), and *Mathematics from the Birth of Numbers* by Jan Gullberg (1997).

Chapter 5

Cartesian Coordinates

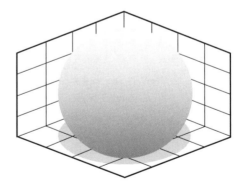

René Descartes (1596–1650) is often credited with the invention of the *xy*-plane, but Pierre de Fermat (1601–1665) was probably the first inventor. In 1636 Fermat was working on a treatise titled *Ad locus planos et solidos isagoge*, which outlined what we now call analytic geometry. Unfortunately, Fermat never published his treatise, although he shared his ideas with other mathematicians such as Blaise Pascal (1623–1662). At the same time Descartes devised his own system of analytic geometry and in 1637 published his results in the prestigious journal *Géométrie*. In the eyes of the scientific world, the publication date of a technical paper determines when a new idea or invention is released into the public domain. Consequently, ever since this publication Descartes has been associated with the *xy*-plane, which is why it is called the *Cartesian plane*. If Fermat had been more efficient in publishing his research results, the *xy*-plane would have been called the Fermatian plane! (Boyer and Merzbach, 1989).

The Cartesian *xy*-plane

The Cartesian *xy*-plane provides a mechanism for translating pairs of related variables into a graphical format. The variables are normally *x* and y, as used to describe a function such as $y = 3x + 2$. Every value of *x* has a corresponding value of *y*, which can be located on intersecting axes as shown in Figure 5.1. The set of points forms a familiar straight line associated with equations of the form $y = mx + c$. By convention, the axis for the independent variable *x* is horizontal, and the dependent variable *y* is vertical. The axes intersect at 90° at a point called the *origin*. As previously mentioned, Descartes suggested that the letters *x* and *y* should be used to represent variables, and letters at the other end of the alphabet should substitute numbers. Which is why equations such as $y = ax^2 + bx + c$ are written the way they are.

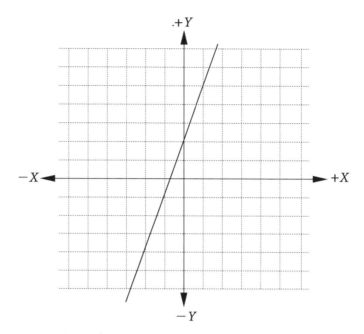

Figure 5.1 *The equation y = 3x + 2*
using the xy Cartesian plane.

Measurements to the right and left of the origin are positive and negative respectively, and measurements above and below the origin share a similar sign convention. Together, the axes are said to create a *left-handed* set of axes, because it is possible, using one's left hand, to align the thumb with the *x*-axis and the first finger with the *y*-axis. We will say more about left and right-handed axes in Chapter 6.

The Cartesian plane is such a simple idea that it is strange it took so long to be discovered. But even though it was invented almost 400 years ago, it is central to computer graphics. However, although it is true that Descartes showed how an orthogonal coordinate system could be used for graphs and coordinate geometry, coordinates had been used by ancient Egyptians, almost 2000 years earlier!

Any point *P* on the Cartesian plane is identified by an ordered pair of numbers (*x*, *y*) where *x* and *y* are called the

Cartesian coordinates of P. Mathematical functions and geometric shapes can then be represented as lists of coordinates inside a program.

Function graphs

A wide variety of functions, such as $y = mx + c$ (linear), $y = ax^2 + bx + c$ (quadratic), $y = ax^3 + bx^2 + cx + d$ (cubic), $y = a \sin(x)$ (trigonometric), etc. create familiar graphs that readily identify the function's origins. Linear functions are straight lines, quadratics are parabolas, cubics have an 's' shape, and trigonometric functions often have a wave-like trace. Such graphs are used in computer animation to control the movement of objects, lights and the virtual camera. But instead of depicting the relationship between x and y, the graphs show the relationship between an activity such as movement, rotation, size, brightness, colour, etc., with time. Figure 5.2 shows an example where the horizontal axis marks the progress of time in animation frames, and the vertical axis records the corresponding brightness of a virtual light source. Such a function forms part of the animator's user interface, and communicates in a very intuitive manner the brightness of the light source for every frame of animation. The animator can then make changes to the function with the aid of interactive software tools.

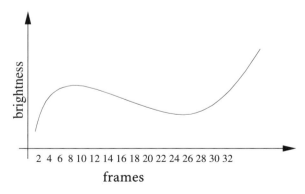

Figure 5.2 A function curve relating brightness to frame number.

Geometric shapes

Computer graphics requires that 2D shapes and 3D objects have a numerical description of some sort. Shapes can include polygons, circles, arbitrary curves, mathematical functions, fractals, etc., and objects can be faceted, smooth, bumpy, furry, gaseous, etc. For the moment, though, we will only consider 2D shapes.

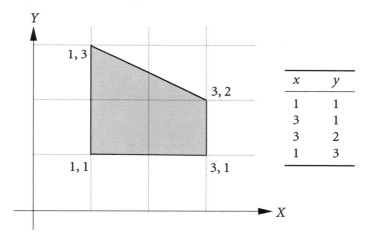

x	y
1	1
3	1
3	2
1	3

Figure 5.3 *A simple polygon created with four vertices shown in the table.*

Polygonal shapes

A polygon is constructed from a sequence of vertices (points) as shown in Figure 5.3. A straight line is assumed to link each pair of neighbouring vertices; intermediate points on the line are not explicitly stored. There is no convention for starting a chain of vertices, but software will often dictate whether polygons have a clockwise or anti-clockwise vertex sequence. If the vertices in Figure 5.3 had been created in an anti-clockwise sequence, they could be represented in a tabular form as shown, where the starting vertex is (1, 1), but this is arbitrary.

We can now subject this list of vertex coordinates to a variety of arithmetic and mathematical operations. For example, if we double the values of x and y and redraw the vertices, we discover that the form of the shape is preserved, but its size is doubled with respect to the origin. Similarly, if we divide the values of x and y by 2, the shape is still preserved, but its size is halved with respect to the origin. On the other hand, if we add 1 to every x-coordinate and 2 to every y-coordinate and redraw the vertices, the shape's size remains the same but it is displaced 1 unit horizontally and 2 units vertically. This arithmetic manipulation of vertices is the basis of shape and object transformations and is described in Chapter 7.

Areas of shapes

The area of a polygonal shape is readily calculated from its chain of coordinates. For example, given the following list of coordinates:

x	y
x_0	y_0
x_1	y_1
x_2	y_2
x_3	y_3

the area is computed by

$$\tfrac{1}{2}[(x_0y_1 - x_1y_0) + (x_1y_2 - x_2y_1) + (x_2y_3 - x_3y_2) + (x_3y_0 - x_0y_3)] \tag{5.1}$$

If you check to see what is happening, you will notice that the calculation sums the results of multiplying an x by the next y, minus the next x by the current y. When the last vertex is selected it is paired with the first vertex to complete the process. The result is then halved to reveal the area.

As a simple test, let's apply (5.1) to the shape described in Figure 5.3:

$$\tfrac{1}{2}\left[(1\times1-3\times1)+(3\times2-3\times1)+(3\times3-1\times2)+(1\times1-1\times3)\right]$$

$$\tfrac{1}{2}\left[-2+3+7-2\right]=3$$

which by inspection, is the true area. The beauty of this technique is that it works with any number of vertices and any arbitrary shape. In Chapter 6 we will discover how it works.

Another feature of the technique is that if the original set of coordinates is clockwise, the area is negative. Which means that the calculation computes vertex sequence as well as area. To illustrate this feature, the original vertices are reversed to a clockwise sequence as follows:

$$\tfrac{1}{2}\left[(1\times3-1\times1)+(1\times2-3\times3)+(3\times1-3\times2)+(3\times1-1\times1)\right]$$

$$\tfrac{1}{2}\left[2-7-3+2\right]=-3$$

The minus sign indicates that the vertices are in a clockwise sequence.

Theorem of Pythagoras in 2D

We can calculate the distance between two points by applying the theorem of Pythagoras. Figure 5.4 shows two arbitrary points $P_1(x_1,y_1)$ and $P_2(x_2,y_2)$. The distance $\Delta x = x_2 - x_1$ and $\Delta y = y_2 - y_1$ Therefore, the distance d between P_1 and P_2 is given by

$$d = \sqrt{\Delta x^2 + \Delta y^2}$$

(5.2)

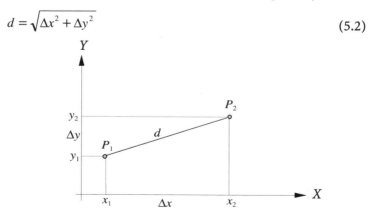

Figure 5.4 *Calculating the distance between two points.*

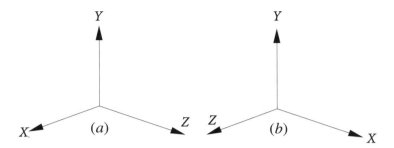

Figure 5.5 *(a) A left-handed system. (b) A right-handed system.*

3D coordinates

In the 2D Cartesian plane a point is located by its x- and y-*coordinates*. But when we move to 3D there are two choices for positioning the third z-axis. Figure 5.5 shows the two possibilities, which are described as *left- and right-handed* axial systems. The left-handed system allows us to align our left hand with the axes such that the thumb aligns with the x-axis, the first finger aligns with the y-axis and the middle finger aligns with the z-axis. The right-handed system allows the same system of alignment, but using our right hand. The choice between these axial systems is arbitrary, but one should be aware of the system employed by commercial computer graphics packages. The main problem arises when projecting 3D points onto a 2D plane, which, in general, has a left-handed axial system. This will become obvious when we look at perspective projections. In this text we will keep to a right-handed system as shown in Figure 5.6, which also shows a point P with its coordinates.

Theorem of Pythagoras in 3D

The theorem of Pythagoras in 3D is a natural extension of the 2D rule. In fact, it even works in higher dimensions. Given two arbitrary points $P_1(x_1, y_1, z_1)$ and $P_2(x_2, y_2, z_2)$, the distance $\Delta x = x_2 - x_1$, $\Delta y = y_2 - y_1$ and $\Delta z = z_2 - z_1$. Therefore, the distance d between P_1 and P_2 is given by

$$d = \sqrt{\Delta x_2 + \Delta y_2 + \Delta z_2} \qquad (5.3)$$

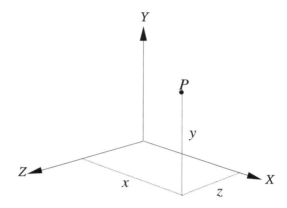

Figure 5.6 *A right-handed axial system showing the coordinates of a point P.*

3D polygons

The simplest 3D polygon is a triangle, which is always *planar*, i.e. the three vertices lie on a unique plane. Planarity is very important in computer graphics because rendering algorithms assume that polygons are planar. For instance, it is quite easy to define a quadrilateral in 3D where the vertices are not located on one plane. When such a polygon is rendered and animated, spurious highlights can result, simply because the geometric techniques (which assume the polygon is planar) give rise to errors.

Euler's rule

In 1619, Descartes discovered quite a nice relationship between vertices, edges and the faces of a 3D polygonal object:

$$faces + vertices = edges + 2 \tag{5.4}$$

As a simple test, consider a cube; it has 12 edges, 6 faces and 8 vertices, which satisfies this equation. This rule can be applied to a geometric database to discover whether it contains any spurious features. Unfortunately for Descartes, for some unknown reason, the rule is named after Euler!

Summary

The Cartesian plane and its associated coordinates are the basis for all mathematics used for computer graphics. We will see in following chapters how shapes can be manipulated using simple functions, and how the plane can be extended into a 3D Cartesian space that becomes the domain for creating objects, curves, surfaces, and a virtual environment where they can be animated and visualized.

Chapter

6

Vectors

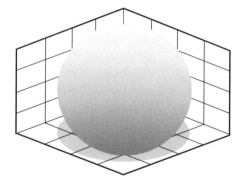

Vectors are a relatively new arrival to the world of mathematics, dating only from the 19th century. They provide us with some elegant and powerful techniques for computing angles between lines and the orientation of surfaces. They also provide a coherent framework for computing the behaviour of dynamic objects in computer animation and illumination models in rendering.

We often employ a single number to represent quantities that we use in our daily lives such as weight, height, age, shoe size, waist and chest measurements. The magnitude of this number depends on our age and whether we use metric or imperial units. Such quantities are called *scalars*. In computer graphics scalar quantities include colour, height, width, depth, brightness, number of frames, etc.

On the other hand, there are some things that require more than one number to represent them: wind, force, velocity and sound are just a few examples. These cannot be represented accurately by a single number. For example, any sailor knows that wind has a magnitude and a direction. The force we use to lift an object also has a value and a direction. Similarly, the velocity of a moving object is measured in terms of its speed (e.g. miles per hour) and a direction such as north-west. Sound, too, has intensity and a direction. These quantities are called *vectors*. In computer graphics, vectors are generally made of two or three numbers, and this is the only type we will consider in this chapter.

Mathematicians such as Caspar Wessel (1745–1818), Jean Argand (1768–1822) and John Warren (1796–1852) were simultaneously exploring complex numbers and their graphical representation. In 1837, Sir William Rowan Hamilton (1788–1856) made his breakthrough with quaternions. In 1853, Hamilton published his book *Lectures on Quaternions* in which he described terms such as *vector*, *transvector* and *provector*. Hamilton's work was not widely accepted until 1881, when the American mathematician Josiah Gibbs (1839–1903) published his treatise *Vector Analysis*, describing modern vector analysis.

2D vectors

In computer graphics we employ 2D and 3D vectors. In this chapter we first consider vector notation in a 2D context and then extrapolate the ideas into 3D.

Vector notation

A scalar such as x is just a name for a single numeric quantity. However, because a vector contains two or more numbers, its symbolic name is printed using a **bold** font to distinguish it from a scalar variable. Examples are **n**, **i** and **Q**.

When a scalar variable is assigned a value we employ the standard algebraic notation

$x = 3$

However, when a vector is assigned its numeric values, the following notation is used:

$$\mathbf{n} = \begin{bmatrix} 3 \\ 4 \end{bmatrix}$$

which is called a *column* vector. The numbers 3 and 4 are called the *components* of **n**, and their position within the brackets is significant. A *row* vector transposes the components horizontally, $\mathbf{n} = [3\ 4]^T$ where the superscript ^{T} reminds us of the transposition.

Graphical representation of vectors

Because vectors have to encode direction as well as magnitude, an arrow could be used to indicate direction and a number to specify magnitude. Such a scheme is often used in weather maps. Although this is a useful graphical interpretation for such data, it is not practical for algebraic manipulation.

Cartesian coordinates provide an excellent mechanism for visualizing vectors and allowing them to be incorporated within the classical framework of mathematics. Figure 6.1 shows a vector represented by a short line segment. The length of the line represents the vector's magnitude, and the orientation defines its direction. But as you can see from the figure, the line does not have a direction. Even if we attach an arrowhead to the line, which is standard practice for annotating vectors in books and scientific papers, the arrowhead has no mathematical reality.

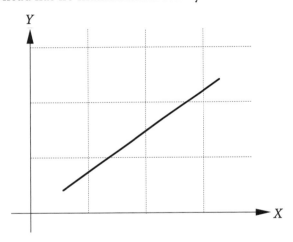

Figure 6.1 *A vector represented by a short line segment. However, although the vector has magnitude, it does not have direction.*

The line's direction can be determined by first identifying the vector's tail and then measuring its components along the x- and y-axes. For example, in Figure 6.2 the vector **r** has its tail defined by $(x_1, y_1) = (1, 2)$ and its head by $(x_2, y_2) = (2, 3)$. Vector **s**, on the other hand, has its tail defined by $(x_3, y_3) = (2, 2)$ and its head by $(x_4, y_4) = (1, 1)$. The x- and y-components for **r** are computed as follows:

$$x_r = (x_2 - x_1) \qquad y_r = (y_2 - y_1)$$
$$x_r = 2 - 1 = 1 \qquad y_r = 3 - 2 = 1$$

whereas the components for **s** are computed as follows:

$$x_s = (x_4 - x_3) \qquad y_s = (y_4 - y_3)$$
$$x_s = 1 - 2 = -1 \quad y_s = 1 - 2 = -1$$
$$x_s = -1 \qquad\qquad y_s = -1$$

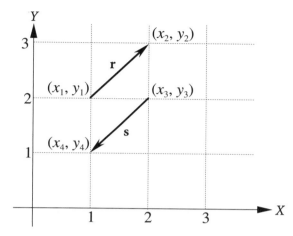

Figure 6.2 *Two vectors* **r** *and* **s** *have the same magnitude and opposite directions.*

It is the negative values of x_s and y_s that encode the vector's direction. In general, given that the coordinates of a vector's head and tail are (x_h, y_h) and (x_t, y_t) respectively, its components Δx and Δy are given by

$$\Delta x = (x_h - x_t) \quad \Delta y = (y_h - y_t) \qquad (6.1)$$

One can readily see from this notation that a vector does not have a unique position in space. It does not matter where we place a vector: so long as we preserve its length and orientation, its components will not alter.

Magnitude of a vector

The *magnitude* of a vector **r** is expressed by $|\mathbf{r}|$ and is computed by applying the theorem of Pythagoras to its components:

$$|\mathbf{r}| = \sqrt{\Delta x^2 + \Delta y^2} \tag{6.2}$$

To illustrate these ideas, consider a vector defined by (x_h, y_h) = (3, 4) and (x_t, y_t) = (1, 1). The x- and y-components are 2 and 3 respectively. Therefore its magnitude is equal to

$$\sqrt{2^2 + 3^2} = 3.606$$

Figure 6.3 shows various vectors, and their properties are listed in Table 6.1.

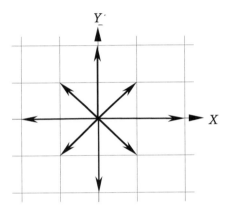

Figure 6.3 *Eight vectors, whose coordinates are shown in Table 6.1.*

Table 6.1 *Values associated with the vectors shown in Fig. 6.3*

x_h	y_h	x_t	y_t	Δx	Δy	|vector|
2	0	0	0	2	0	2
0	2	0	0	0	2	2
−2	0	0	0	−2	0	2
0	−2	0	0	0	−2	2
1	1	0	0	1	1	$\sqrt{2}$
−1	1	0	0	−1	1	$\sqrt{2}$
−1	−1	0	0	−1	−1	$\sqrt{2}$
1	−1	0	0	1	−1	$\sqrt{2}$

3D vectors

The above vector examples are in 2D, but it is extremely simple to extend this notation to embrace an extra dimension. Figure 6.4 shows a 3D vector **r** with its head, tail, components and magnitude annotated. The components and magnitude are given by

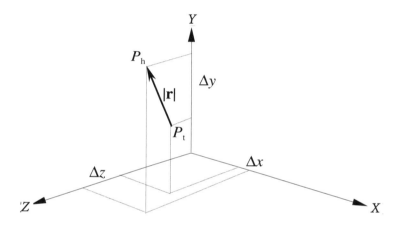

Figure 6.4 *The 3D vector has components Δx, Δy, Δz, which are the differences between the head and tail coordinates.*

$$\Delta x = (x_h - x_t) \tag{6.3}$$

$$\Delta y = (y_h - y_t) \tag{6.4}$$

$$\Delta z = (z_h - z_t) \tag{6.5}$$

$$|\mathbf{r}| = \sqrt{\Delta x^2 + \Delta y^2 + \Delta z^2} \tag{6.6}$$

As 3D vectors play a very important part in computer animation, all future examples will be three-dimensional.

Vector manipulation

As vectors are different from scalars, a set of rules has been developed to control how the two mathematical entities interact with one another. For instance, we need to consider vector addition, subtraction and multiplication, and how a vector can be modified by a scalar. Let's begin with multiplying a vector by a scalar.

Multiplying a vector by a scalar

Given a vector **n**, 2**n** means that the vector's components are doubled. For example, if

$$\mathbf{n} = \begin{bmatrix} 3 \\ 4 \\ 5 \end{bmatrix} \quad \text{then} \quad 2\mathbf{n} = \begin{bmatrix} 6 \\ 8 \\ 10 \end{bmatrix}$$

which seems logical. Similarly, if we divide **n** by 2, its components are halved. Note that the vector's direction remains unchanged – only its magnitude changes.

It is meaningless to consider the addition of a scalar to a vector such as **n** + 2, for it is not obvious which component of **n** is to be increased by 2. If all the components of **n** have to be increased by 2, then we simply add another vector whose components equal 2.

Vector addition and subtraction

Given vectors **r** and **s**, **r** ± **s** is defined as

$$\mathbf{r} = \begin{bmatrix} x_r \\ y_r \\ z_r \end{bmatrix} \qquad \mathbf{s} = \begin{bmatrix} x_s \\ y_s \\ z_s \end{bmatrix} \qquad \mathbf{r} \pm \mathbf{s} = \begin{bmatrix} x_r \pm x_s \\ y_r \pm y_s \\ z_r \pm z_s \end{bmatrix} \qquad (6.7)$$

Vector addition is commutative:

$$\mathbf{a} + \mathbf{b} = \mathbf{b} + \mathbf{a} \qquad (6.8)$$

e.g. $\begin{bmatrix} 1 \\ 2 \\ 3 \end{bmatrix} + \begin{bmatrix} 4 \\ 5 \\ 6 \end{bmatrix} = \begin{bmatrix} 4 \\ 5 \\ 6 \end{bmatrix} + \begin{bmatrix} 1 \\ 2 \\ 3 \end{bmatrix} = \begin{bmatrix} 5 \\ 7 \\ 9 \end{bmatrix}$

However, like scalar subtraction, vector subtraction is not commutative:

$$\mathbf{a} - \mathbf{b} \neq \mathbf{b} - \mathbf{a}$$

e.g.
$$\begin{bmatrix} 4 \\ 5 \\ 6 \end{bmatrix} - \begin{bmatrix} 1 \\ 2 \\ 3 \end{bmatrix} \neq \begin{bmatrix} 1 \\ 2 \\ 3 \end{bmatrix} - \begin{bmatrix} 4 \\ 5 \\ 6 \end{bmatrix}$$

$$\mathbf{a} - \mathbf{b} \neq \mathbf{b} - \mathbf{a} \tag{6.9}$$

Let's illustrate vector addition and subtraction with two examples. Figure 6.5 shows the graphical interpretation of adding two vectors $\mathbf{r}$ and $\mathbf{s}$. Note that the tail of vector $\mathbf{s}$ is attached to the head of vector $\mathbf{r}$. The resultant vector $\mathbf{t} = \mathbf{r} + \mathbf{s}$ is defined by adding the corresponding components of $\mathbf{r}$ and $\mathbf{s}$ together. Figure 6.6 shows a graphical interpretation for $\mathbf{r} - \mathbf{s}$. This time the components of vector $\mathbf{s}$ are reversed to produce an equal and opposite vector. Then it is attached to $\mathbf{r}$ and added as described above.

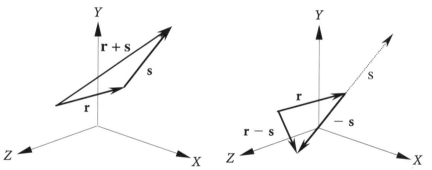

Figure 6.5 *Vector addition* $\mathbf{r} + \mathbf{s}$.   **Figure 6.6** *Vector subtraction* $\mathbf{r} - \mathbf{s}$.

Position vectors

Given any point $P(x, y, z)$, a *position* vector $\mathbf{p}$ can be created by assuming that P is the vector's head and the origin is its tail. Because the tail coordinates are $(0, 0, 0)$ the vector's components are x, y, z. Consequently, the vector's magnitude $|\mathbf{p}|$ equals $\sqrt{x^2 + y^2 + z^2}$. For example, the point $P(4, 5, 6)$ creates a position vector $\mathbf{p}$ relative to the origin:

$$\mathbf{p} = \begin{bmatrix} 4 \\ 5 \\ 6 \end{bmatrix} \qquad |\mathbf{p}| = \sqrt{4^2 + 5^2 + 6^2} = 20.88$$

We will see how position vectors are used in Chapter 8 when we consider analytical geometry.

Unit vectors

By definition, a *unit* vector has a magnitude of 1. A simple example is **i** where

$$\mathbf{i} = \begin{bmatrix} 1 \\ 0 \\ 0 \end{bmatrix} \qquad |\mathbf{i}| = 1$$

Unit vectors are extremely useful when we come to vector multiplication. As we shall discover later, multiplication of vectors involves taking their magnitude, and if this is unity, the multiplication is greatly simplified. Furthermore, in computer graphics applications vectors are used to specify the orientation of surfaces, the direction of light sources and the virtual camera. Again, if these vectors have a unit length, the computation time associated with vector operations can be minimized.

Converting a vector into a unit form is called *normalizing* and is achieved by dividing a vector's components by its magnitude. To formalize this process, consider a vector **r** whose components are *x*, *y*, *z*. The magnitude $|\mathbf{r}| = \sqrt{x^2 + y^2 + z^2}$ and the unit form of **r** are given by

$$\mathbf{r}_\mathrm{u} = \frac{1}{|\mathbf{r}|} \begin{bmatrix} x \\ y \\ z \end{bmatrix} \qquad (6.10)$$

This process can be confirmed by showing that the magnitude of $\mathbf{r}_\mathrm{u}$ is 1:

$$|\mathbf{r}_u| = \sqrt{\left(\frac{x}{|\mathbf{r}|}\right)^2 + \left(\frac{y}{|\mathbf{r}|}\right)^2 + \left(\frac{z}{|\mathbf{r}|}\right)^2}$$

$$= \frac{1}{|\mathbf{r}|}\sqrt{x^2 + y^2 + z^2} = 1$$

To put this into context, consider the conversion of $\mathbf{r}$ into a unit form:

$$\mathbf{r} = \begin{bmatrix} 1 \\ 2 \\ 3 \end{bmatrix}$$

$$|\mathbf{r}| = \sqrt{1^2 + 2^2 + 3^2} \qquad = \sqrt{14}$$

$$\mathbf{r}_u = \frac{1}{\sqrt{14}}\begin{bmatrix} 1 \\ 2 \\ 3 \end{bmatrix} \qquad = \begin{bmatrix} 0.267 \\ 0.535 \\ 0.802 \end{bmatrix}$$

Cartesian vectors

Now that we have considered the scalar multiplication of vectors, vector addition and unit vectors, we can combine all three to permit the algebraic manipulation of vectors. To begin with, we will define three Cartesian unit vectors $\mathbf{i}$, $\mathbf{j}$, $\mathbf{k}$ that are aligned with the x-, y- and z-axes respectively:

$$\mathbf{i} = \begin{bmatrix} 1 \\ 0 \\ 0 \end{bmatrix}, \qquad \mathbf{j} = \begin{bmatrix} 0 \\ 1 \\ 0 \end{bmatrix}, \qquad \mathbf{k} = \begin{bmatrix} 0 \\ 0 \\ 1 \end{bmatrix} \qquad (6.11)$$

Therefore any vector aligned with the x-, y- or z-axes can be defined by a scalar multiple of the unit vectors $\mathbf{i}$, $\mathbf{j}$ and $\mathbf{k}$ respectively. For example, a vector 10 units long aligned with the x-axis is simply $10\mathbf{i}$, and a vector 20 units long aligned with the z-axis is $20\mathbf{k}$. By employing the rules of vector addition and subtraction, we can compose a vector **r** by adding three *Cartesian* vectors as follows:

$$\mathbf{r} = a\mathbf{i} + b\mathbf{j} + c\mathbf{k} \tag{6.12}$$

This is equivalent to writing **r** as

$$\mathbf{r} = \begin{bmatrix} a \\ b \\ c \end{bmatrix} \tag{6.13}$$

which means that the magnitude of **r** is readily computed as

$$|\mathbf{r}| = \sqrt{a^2 + b^2 + c^2} \tag{6.14}$$

Any pair of Cartesian vectors such as **r** and **s** can be combined as follows:

$$\mathbf{r} = a\mathbf{i} + b\mathbf{j} + c\mathbf{k} \tag{6.15}$$

$$\mathbf{s} = d\mathbf{i} + e\mathbf{j} + f\mathbf{k} \tag{6.16}$$

$$\mathbf{r} \pm \mathbf{s} = (a \pm d)\mathbf{i} + (b \pm e)\mathbf{j} + (c \pm f)\mathbf{k} \tag{6.17}$$

For example, given

$$\mathbf{r} = 2\mathbf{i} + 3\mathbf{j} + 4\mathbf{k} \text{ and } \mathbf{s} = 5\mathbf{i} + 6\mathbf{j} + 7\mathbf{k}$$

then $\mathbf{r} + \mathbf{s} = 7\mathbf{i} + 9\mathbf{j} + 11\mathbf{k}$

and

$$|\mathbf{r} + \mathbf{s}| = \sqrt{7^2 + 9^2 + 11^2} \qquad = \sqrt{251} \qquad = 15.84$$

Vector multiplication

Although vector addition and subtraction are useful in resolving various problems, vector multiplication provides some powerful ways of computing angles and surface orientations.

The multiplication of two scalars is very familiar: for example, 6×7 or $7 \times 6 = 42$. We often visualize this operation, as a rectangular area where 6 and 7 are the dimensions of a rectangle's sides, and 42 is the area. However, when we consider the multiplication of vectors we are basically multiplying two 3D lines together, which is not an easy operation to visualize.

Mathematicians have discovered that there are two ways to multiply vectors together: one gives rise to a scalar result and the other a vector result. We will start with the *scalar product*.

Scalar product

We could multiply two vectors **r** and **s** by using the product of their magnitudes: $|\mathbf{r}| \cdot |\mathbf{s}|$. Although this is a valid operation, it does not get us anywhere because it ignores the orientation of the vectors, which is one of their important features. The concept, however, is readily developed into a useful operation by including the angle between the vectors.

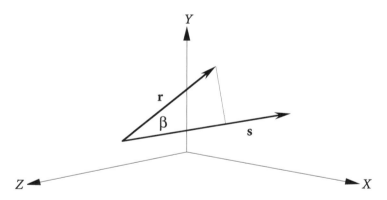

Figure 6.7 *The projection of* **r** *on* **s** *creates the basis for the scaler product.*

Figure 6.7 shows two vectors **r** and **s** that have been drawn, for convenience, such that their tails touch. Taking **s** as the reference vector, which is an arbitrary choice, we compute the projection of **r** on **s**, which takes into account their relative orientation. The length of **r** on **s** is $|\mathbf{r}|\cos(\beta)$. We can now multiply the magnitude of **s** by the projected length of **r**: $|\mathbf{s}| \cdot |\mathbf{r}|\cos(\beta)$. This scalar product is written

$$s \cdot r = |s| \cdot |r| \cos(\beta) \qquad (6.18)$$

The dot symbol '·' is used to represent scalar multiplication, to distinguish it from the vector product, which, we will discover, employs a '×' symbol. Because of this symbol, the scalar product is often referred to as the *dot product*.

So far we have only defined what we mean by the dot product. We now need to find out how to compute it. Fortunately, everything is in place to perform this task. To begin with, we define two Cartesian vectors **r** and **s**, and proceed to multiply them together using the dot product definition:

$$r = ai + bj + ck \qquad (6.19)$$

$$s = di + ej + fk \qquad (6.20)$$

therefore

$$r \cdot s = (ai + bj + ck) \cdot (di + ej + fk)$$
$$= ai \cdot (di + ej + fk) +$$
$$bj \cdot (di + ej + fk) +$$
$$ck \cdot (di + ej + fk)$$
$$r \cdot s = ad(i \cdot i) + ae(i \cdot j) + af(i \cdot k) +$$
$$bd(j \cdot i) + be(j \cdot j) + bf(j \cdot k) +$$
$$cd(k \cdot i) + ce(k \cdot j) + cf(k \cdot k) \qquad (6.21)$$

Before we proceed any further, we can see that we have created various dot product terms such as $(i \cdot i)$, $(j \cdot j)$, $(k \cdot k)$, etc. These terms can be divided into two groups: those that involve the same unit vector, and those that reference different unit vectors.

Using the definition of the dot product, terms such as $(i \cdot i)$, $(j \cdot j)$ and $(k \cdot k) = 1$, because the angle between **i** and **i**, **j** and **j**, or **k** and **k** is 0°; and $\cos(0°) = 1$. But because the other vector combinations are separated by 90°, and $\cos(90°) = 0$, all remaining terms collapse to zero. Bearing in mind that the magnitude of a unit vector is 1, we can write

$$|s| \cdot |r| \cos(\beta) = ad + be + cf \qquad (6.22)$$

This result confirms that the dot product is indeed a scalar quantity. Now let's see how it works in practice.

Example of the dot product

To find the angle between two vectors **r** and **s**,

$$\mathbf{r} = \begin{bmatrix} 2 \\ -3 \\ 4 \end{bmatrix} \quad \text{and} \quad \mathbf{s} = \begin{bmatrix} 5 \\ 6 \\ 10 \end{bmatrix}$$

$$|\mathbf{r}| = \sqrt{2^2 + (-3)^2 + 4^2} \quad = 5.385$$

$$|\mathbf{s}| = \sqrt{5^2 + 6^2 + 10^2} \quad = 12.689$$

Therefore

$$|\mathbf{s}| \cdot |\mathbf{r}| \cos(\beta) = 2 \times 5 + (-3) \times 6 + 4 \times 10 = 32$$

$$12.689 \times 5.385 \times \cos(\beta) = 32$$

$$\cos(\beta) = \frac{32}{12.689 \times 5.385} \quad = 0.468$$

$$\beta = \cos^{-1}(0.468) = 62.1°$$

The angle between the two vectors is 62.1°.

It is worth pointing out at this stage that the angle returned by the dot product ranges between 0° and 180°. This is because, as the angle between two vectors increases beyond 180°, the returned angle β is always the smallest angle associated with the geometry.

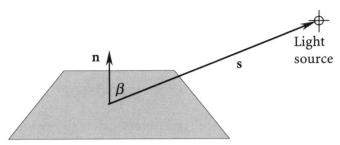

Figure 6.8 *Lambert's law states that the intensity of illumination on a diffuse surface is proportional to the cosine of the angle between the surface normal vector and the light source direction.*

The dot product in lighting calculations

Lambert's law states that the intensity of illumination on a diffuse surface is proportional to the cosine of the angle between the surface normal vector and the light source direction. This arrangement is shown in Figure 6.8. The light source is located at $(20, 20, 40)$ and the illuminated point is $(0, 10, 0)$.

In this situation we are interested in calculating $\cos(\beta)$, which when multiplied by the light source intensity gives the incident light intensity on the surface. To begin with, we are given the normal vector **n** to the surface. In this case **n** is a unit vector, and its magnitude $|\mathbf{n}| = 1$:

$$\mathbf{n} = \begin{bmatrix} 0 \\ 1 \\ 0 \end{bmatrix}$$

The direction of the light source from the surface is defined by the vector **s**:

$$\mathbf{s} = \begin{bmatrix} 20-0 \\ 20-10 \\ 40-0 \end{bmatrix} = \begin{bmatrix} 20 \\ 10 \\ 40 \end{bmatrix}$$

$$|\mathbf{s}| = \sqrt{20^2 + 10^2 + 40^2} = 45.826$$

$$|\mathbf{n}| \cdot |\mathbf{s}|\cos(\beta) = 0 \times 20 + 1 \times 10 + 0 \times 40 = 10$$

$$1 \times 45.826 \times \cos(\beta) = 10$$

$$\cos(\beta) = \frac{10}{45.826} = 0.218$$

Therefore the light intensity at the point $(0, 10, 0)$ is 0.218 of the original light intensity at $(20, 20, 40)$. This does not take into account the attenuation due to the inverse-square law of light propagation.

The dot product in back-face detection

A standard way of identifying back-facing polygons relative to the virtual camera is to compute the angle between the polygon's surface normal and the line of sight between the camera and the polygon. If this angle is less than 90° the polygon is visible; if it is equal to or greater than 90° the polygon is invisible. This geometry is shown in Figure 6.9. Although it is obvious from Figure 6.9 that the right-hand polygon is invisible to the camera, let's prove algebraically that this is so. Let the camera be located at $(0,0,0)$ and the polygon's vertex is $(10, 10, 40)$. The normal vector is $[5\ 5\ -2]^{\mathrm{T}}$.

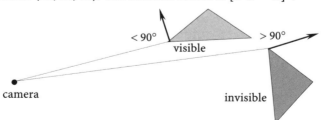

Figure 6.9 *The angle between the surface normal and the camera's line of sight determines the polygon's visibility.*

$$n = \begin{bmatrix} 5 \\ 5 \\ -2 \end{bmatrix}$$

$$|n| = \sqrt{5^2 + 5^2 + (-2)^2} \qquad = 7.348$$

The camera vector **c** is

$$c = \begin{bmatrix} 0-10 \\ 0-10 \\ 0-40 \end{bmatrix} \qquad = \begin{bmatrix} -10 \\ -10 \\ -40 \end{bmatrix}$$

$$|c| = \sqrt{(-10)^2 + (-10)^2 + (-40)^2} \qquad = 42.426$$

therefore

$$|n| \cdot |c| \cos(\beta) = 5 \times (-10) + 5 \times (-10) + (-2) \times (-40)$$

$$7.348 \times 42.426 \times \cos(\beta) = -20$$

$$\cos(\beta) = \frac{-20}{7.348 \times 42.426} \qquad = -0.0634$$

$$\beta = \cos^{-1}(-0.0634) = 93.635°$$

which shows that the polygon is invisible.

The vector product

As mentioned above, there are two ways to obtain the product of two vectors. The first is the scalar product, and the second is the *vector product*, which is also called the *cross product* because of the '×' symbol used in its notation. It is based on the definition that two vectors **r** and **s** can be multiplied together to produce a third vector **t**:

$$r \times s = t \qquad (6.23)$$

where $|t| = |r| \cdot |s| \sin(\beta)$, and β is the angle between **r** and **s**.

We will discover that the vector **t** is normal (90°) to the plane containing the vectors **r** and **s**. This makes it an ideal way of computing the surface normal to a polygon. Once again, let's define two vectors and proceed to multiply them together:

$$\mathbf{r} = a\mathbf{i} + b\mathbf{j} + c\mathbf{k} \tag{6.24}$$

$$\mathbf{s} = d\mathbf{i} + e\mathbf{j} + f\mathbf{k} \tag{6.25}$$

$$\mathbf{r} \times \mathbf{s} = (a\mathbf{i} + b\mathbf{j} + c\mathbf{k}) \times (d\mathbf{i} + e\mathbf{j} + f\mathbf{k})$$

$$= a\mathbf{i} \times (d\mathbf{i} + e\mathbf{j} + f\mathbf{k}) + b\mathbf{j} \times (d\mathbf{i} + e\mathbf{j} + f\mathbf{k}) + c\mathbf{k} \times (d\mathbf{i} + e\mathbf{j} + f\mathbf{k})$$

$$\mathbf{r} \times \mathbf{s} = ad(\mathbf{i} \times \mathbf{i}) + ae(\mathbf{i} \times \mathbf{j}) + af(\mathbf{i} \times \mathbf{k}) + bd(\mathbf{j} \times \mathbf{i}) + be(\mathbf{j} \times \mathbf{j}) + bf(\mathbf{j} \times \mathbf{k}) + cd(\mathbf{k} \times \mathbf{i}) + ce(\mathbf{k} \times \mathbf{j}) + cf(\mathbf{k} \times \mathbf{k}) \tag{6.26}$$

As we found with the dot product, there are two groups of vector terms: those that reference the same unit vector, and those that reference two different unit vectors.

Using the definition for the cross product, operations such as $(\mathbf{i} \times \mathbf{i}), (\mathbf{j} \times \mathbf{j})$ and $(\mathbf{k} \times \mathbf{k})$ result in a vector whose magnitude is 0. This is because the angle between the vectors is 0°, and $\sin(0°) = 0$. Consequently these terms disappear and we are left with

$$\mathbf{r} \times \mathbf{s} = ae(\mathbf{i} \times \mathbf{j}) + af(\mathbf{i} \times \mathbf{k}) + bd(\mathbf{j} \times \mathbf{i}) + bf(\mathbf{j} \times \mathbf{k}) + cd(\mathbf{k} \times \mathbf{i}) + ce(\mathbf{k} \times \mathbf{j}) \tag{6.27}$$

The mathematician Sir William Rowan Hamilton struggled for many years when working on quaternions to resolve the meaning of the above result. What did the products mean? He assumed that $\mathbf{i} \times \mathbf{j} = \mathbf{k}, \mathbf{j} \times \mathbf{k} = \mathbf{i}$ and $\mathbf{k} \times \mathbf{i} = \mathbf{j}$, but he also thought that $\mathbf{j} \times \mathbf{i} = \mathbf{k}, \mathbf{k} \times \mathbf{j} = \mathbf{i}$ and $\mathbf{i} \times \mathbf{k} = \mathbf{j}$. But this did not work! One day in 1843, when he was out walking, thinking about this problem, he thought the impossible: $\mathbf{i} \times \mathbf{j} = \mathbf{k}$, but $\mathbf{j} \times \mathbf{i} = -\mathbf{k}, \mathbf{j} \times \mathbf{k} = \mathbf{i}$, but $\mathbf{k} \times \mathbf{j} = -\mathbf{i}$, and $\mathbf{k} \times \mathbf{i} = \mathbf{j}$, but $\mathbf{i} \times \mathbf{k} = -\mathbf{j}$. To his surprise, this worked, but it contradicted the commutative multiplication law of scalars where $6 \times 7 = 7 \times 6$. We now accept that vectors do not obey all the rules of scalars, which is an interesting result.

Proceeding, then, with Hamilton's rules, we reduce the cross product terms of (6.27) to

$$\mathbf{r} \times \mathbf{s} = ae(\mathbf{k}) + af(-\mathbf{j}) + bd(-\mathbf{k}) + bf(\mathbf{i}) + cd(\mathbf{j}) + ce(-\mathbf{i})$$

$$= (bf - ce)\mathbf{i} + (cd - af)\mathbf{j} + (ae - bd)\mathbf{k} \qquad (6.28)$$

We now modify the middle term to create a symmetric result:

$$\mathbf{r} \times \mathbf{s} = (bf - ce)\mathbf{i} - (af - cd)\mathbf{j} + (ae - bd)\mathbf{k} \qquad (6.29)$$

If this is written in determinant form we get

$$\mathbf{r} \times \mathbf{s} = \begin{vmatrix} b & c \\ e & f \end{vmatrix} \mathbf{i} - \begin{vmatrix} a & c \\ d & f \end{vmatrix} \mathbf{j} + \begin{vmatrix} a & b \\ d & e \end{vmatrix} \mathbf{k} \qquad (6.30)$$

where the *determinants* provide the scalar for each unit vector. We will discover later that the determinant of a 2×2 matrix is the difference between the products of the diagonal terms.

Although it may not be obvious, there is a simple elegance to this result, which enables the cross product to be calculated very quickly. To derive the cross product we write the vectors in the correct sequence. Remember that $\mathbf{r} \times \mathbf{s}$ does not equal $\mathbf{s} \times \mathbf{r}$. First take $\mathbf{r} \times \mathbf{s}$:

$$\mathbf{r} = a\mathbf{i} + b\mathbf{j} + c\mathbf{k}$$

$$\mathbf{s} = d\mathbf{i} + e\mathbf{j} + f\mathbf{k} \qquad (6.31)$$

The scalar multiplier for $\mathbf{i}$ is $(bf - ec)$. This is found by ignoring the $\mathbf{i}$ components and looking at the scalar multipliers of $\mathbf{j}$ and $\mathbf{k}$.

The scalar multiplier for $-\mathbf{j}$ is $(af - dc)$. This is found by ignoring the $\mathbf{j}$ components and looking at the $\mathbf{i}$ and $\mathbf{k}$ scalars.

The scalar multiplier for $\mathbf{k}$ is $(ae - db)$. This is found by ignoring the $\mathbf{k}$ components and looking at the $\mathbf{i}$ and $\mathbf{j}$ scalars.

Let's illustrate this with some examples. First we confirm that the vector product works with the unit vectors $\mathbf{i}, \mathbf{j}$ and $\mathbf{k}$:

$$\mathbf{i} = 1\mathbf{i} + 0\mathbf{j} + 0\mathbf{k}$$

$$\mathbf{j} = 0\mathbf{i} + 1\mathbf{j} + 0\mathbf{k}$$

$$\mathbf{k} = 0\mathbf{i} + 0\mathbf{j} + 1\mathbf{k}$$

Therefore

$$\mathbf{i} \times \mathbf{j} = (0 \times 0 - 1 \times 0)\mathbf{i} - (1 \times 0 - 0 \times 0)\mathbf{j} + (1 \times 1 - 0 \times 0)\mathbf{k}$$

$$= 0\mathbf{i} - 0\mathbf{j} + 1\mathbf{k}$$

$$= \mathbf{k}$$

$$\mathbf{j} \times \mathbf{k} = (1 \times 1 - 0 \times 0)\mathbf{i} - (0 \times 1 - 0 \times 0)\mathbf{j} + (0 \times 0 - 0 \times 1)\mathbf{k}$$

$$= 1\mathbf{i} - 0\mathbf{j} + 0\mathbf{k}$$

$$= \mathbf{i}$$

$$\mathbf{k} \times \mathbf{i} = (0 \times 0 - 0 \times 1)\mathbf{i} - (0 \times 0 - 1 \times 1)\mathbf{j} + (0 \times 0 - 1 \times 0)\mathbf{k}$$

$$= 0\mathbf{i} + 1\mathbf{j} + 0\mathbf{k}$$

$$= \mathbf{j}$$

Table 6.2 *Coordinates of the vertices used in Fig. 6.10.*

Vertex	x	y	z
v_1	0	0	1
v_2	1	0	0
v_3	0	1	0

Let's now consider two vectors **r** and **s** and compute the normal vector **t**. The vectors will be chosen so that we can anticipate approximately the answer. Figure 6.10 shows the vectors **r** and **s** and the normal vector **t**. Table 6.2 contains the coordinates of the vertices forming the two vectors.

$$\mathbf{r} = \begin{bmatrix} x_3 - x_2 \\ y_3 - y_2 \\ z_3 - z_2 \end{bmatrix} \qquad \mathbf{s} = \begin{bmatrix} x_1 - x_2 \\ y_1 - y_2 \\ z_1 - z_2 \end{bmatrix}$$

$$\mathbf{r} = -1\mathbf{i} + 1\mathbf{j} + 0\mathbf{k}$$

$$\mathbf{s} = -1\mathbf{i} + 0\mathbf{j} + 1\mathbf{k}$$

$$\mathbf{r} \times \mathbf{s} = (1 \times 1 - 0 \times 0)\mathbf{i} - (-1 \times 1 - (-1) \times 0)\mathbf{j} + (-1 \times 0 - (-1) \times 1)\mathbf{k}$$

$$= 1\mathbf{i} + 1\mathbf{j} + 1\mathbf{k}$$

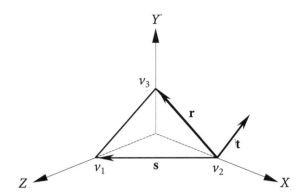

Figure 6.10 *The vector **t** is normal to the vectors **r** and **s**.*

This confirms what we expected from Figure 6.10. Let's now reverse the vectors to illustrate the importance of vector sequence:

$$\mathbf{s} = -1\mathbf{i} + 0\mathbf{j} + 1\mathbf{k}$$

$$\mathbf{r} = -1\mathbf{i} + 1\mathbf{j} + 0\mathbf{k}$$

$$\mathbf{s} \times \mathbf{r} = (0 \times 0 - 1 \times 1)\mathbf{i} - (-1 \times 0 - (-1) \times 1)\mathbf{j} +$$
$$(-1 \times 1 - (-1) \times 0)\mathbf{k}$$

$$= -1\mathbf{i} - 1\mathbf{j} - 1\mathbf{k}$$

which is in the opposite direction to $\mathbf{r} \times \mathbf{s}$.

The right-hand rule

The *right-hand rule* is an *aide mémoire* for working out the orientation of the cross product vector. Given the operation $\mathbf{r} \times \mathbf{s}$, if the right-hand thumb is aligned with $\mathbf{r}$, the first finger with $\mathbf{s}$, and the middle finger points in the direction of $\mathbf{t}$.

Deriving a unit normal vector for a triangle

Figure 6.11 shows a triangle with vertices defined in an anti-clockwise sequence from its visible side. This is the side we want the surface normal to point upwards. Using the following information we will compute the surface normal using the cross product and then convert it to a unit normal vector.

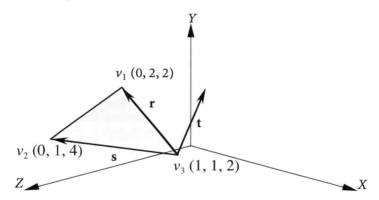

Figure 6.11 *The normal vector* **t** *is derived from the cross product* **r** × **s.**

Create vector **r** between v_1 and v_3, and vector **s** between v_2 and v_3:

$\mathbf{r} = -1\mathbf{i} + 1\mathbf{j} + 0\mathbf{k}$

$\mathbf{s} = -1\mathbf{i} + 0\mathbf{j} + 2\mathbf{k}$

$\mathbf{r} \times \mathbf{s} = \mathbf{t} = (1 \times 2 - 0 \times 0)\mathbf{i} - (-1 \times 2 - 0 \times -1)\mathbf{j} + (-1 \times 0 - 1 \times -1)\mathbf{k}$

$\mathbf{t} = 2\mathbf{i} + 2\mathbf{j} + 1\mathbf{k}$

$|\mathbf{t}| = \sqrt{2^2 + 2^2 + 1^2} \qquad = 3$

$\mathbf{t}_u = \frac{2}{3}\mathbf{i} + \frac{2}{3}\mathbf{j} + \frac{1}{3}\mathbf{k}$

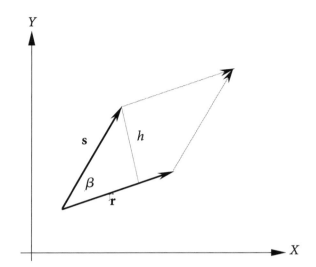

*Figure 6.12 The area of the parallelogram formed by two vectors **r** and **s** equals $|\mathbf{r}| \cdot |\mathbf{s}|\sin(\beta)$.*

The unit vector $\mathbf{t_u}$ can now be used in illumination calculations, and as it has unit length, dot product calculations are simplified.

Areas

Before we leave the cross product let's investigate the physical meaning of $|\mathbf{r}| \cdot |\mathbf{s}|\sin(\beta)$. Figure 6.12 shows two 2D vectors, $\mathbf{r}$ and $\mathbf{s}$. The height $h = |\mathbf{s}|\sin(\beta)$, therefore the area of the parallelogram is

$$|\mathbf{r}|h = |\mathbf{r}| \cdot |\mathbf{s}|\sin(\beta) \tag{6.32}$$

But this is the magnitude of the cross product vector $\mathbf{t}$. Thus when we calculate $\mathbf{r} \times \mathbf{s}$, the length of the normal vector $\mathbf{t}$ equals the area of the parallelogram formed by $\mathbf{r}$ and $\mathbf{s}$. Which means that the triangle formed by halving the parallelogram is half the area.

$$\text{area of parallelogram} = |\mathbf{t}| \tag{6.33}$$

$$\text{area of triangle} = \tfrac{1}{2}|\mathbf{t}| \tag{6.34}$$

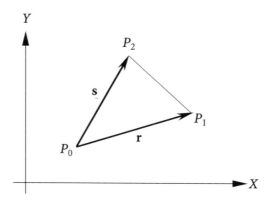

Figure 6.13 *The area of the triangle formed by the vectors* **r** *and* **s** *is half the magnitude of their cross product.*

This means that it is a relatively easy exercise to calculate the surface area of an object constructed from triangles or parallelograms. In the case of a triangulated surface, we simply sum the magnitudes of the normals and halve the result.

Calculating 2D areas

Figure 6.13 shows three vertices of a triangle $P_0(x_0, y_0)$, $P_1(x_1, y_1)$ and $P_2(x_2, y_2)$ formed in an anti-clockwise sequence. We can imagine that the triangle exists on the $z = 0$ plane, therefore the *z-coordinates* are zero.

The vectors **r** and **s** are computed as follows:

$$\mathbf{r} = \begin{bmatrix} x_1 - x_0 \\ y_1 - y_0 \\ 0 \end{bmatrix} \qquad \mathbf{s} = \begin{bmatrix} x_2 - x_0 \\ y_2 - y_0 \\ 0 \end{bmatrix} \tag{6.35}$$

$$\mathbf{r} = (x_1 - x_0)\mathbf{i} + (y_1 - y_0)\mathbf{j} + 0\mathbf{k} \tag{6.36}$$

$$\mathbf{s} = (x_2 - x_0)\mathbf{i} + (y_2 - y_0)\mathbf{j} + 0\mathbf{k} \tag{6.37}$$

$$|\mathbf{r} \times \mathbf{s}| = (x_1 - x_0)(y_2 - y_0) - (x_2 - x_0)(y_1 - y_0)$$

$$= x_1(y_2 - y_0) - x_0(y_2 - y_0) - x_2(y_1 - y_0) + x_0(y_1 - y_0)$$

$$= x_1 y_2 - x_1 y_0 - x_0 y_2 - x_0 y_0 - x_2 y_1 + x_2 y_0 + x_0 y_1 - x_0 y_0$$

$$= x_1 y_2 - x_1 y_0 - x_0 y_2 - x_2 y_1 + x_2 y_0 + x_0 y_1$$

$$= (x_0 y_1 - x_1 y_0) + (x_1 y_2 - x_2 y_1) + (x_2 y_0 - x_0 y_2) \quad (6.38)$$

But the area of the triangle formed by the three vertices is $\frac{1}{2}|\mathbf{r} \times \mathbf{s}|$. Therefore

$$\text{area} = \frac{1}{2} [= (x_0 y_1 - x_1 y_0) + (x_1 y_2 - x_2 y_1) + (x_2 y_0 - x_0 y_2) \quad (6.39)$$

which is the formula disclosed in Chapter 2!

Summary

Even if you already knew something about vectors, I hope this chapter has introduced some new ideas and illustrated the role vectors play in computer graphics.

Chapter

7

Transformations

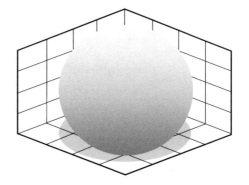

Transformations are used to scale, translate, rotate, reflect and shear shapes and objects. And, as we shall discover shortly, it is possible to effect this by changing their coordinate values.

Although algebra is the basic notation for transformations, it is also possible to express them as *matrices*, which provide certain advantages for viewing the transformation and for interfacing to various types of computer graphics hardware. We begin with an algebraic approach and then introduce matrix notation.

2D transformations

Translation

Cartesian coordinates provide a one-to-one relationship between number and shape, such that when we change a shape's coordinates, we change its geometry. For example, if $P(x, y)$ is a vertex on a shape, when we apply the operation $x' = x + 3$ we create a new point $P'(x', y)$ three units to the right. Similarly, the operation $y' = y + 1$ creates a new point $P'(x, y')$ displaced one unit vertically. By applying both of these transforms to every vertex to the original shape, the shape is displaced as shown in Figure 7.1.

Scaling

Shape scaling is achieved by multiplying coordinates as follows:

$$x' = 2x$$

$$y' = 1.5y \tag{7.1}$$

This transform results in a horizontal scaling of 2 and a vertical scaling of 1.5, as illustrated in Figure 7.2. Note that a point located at the origin does not change its place, so scaling is relative to the origin.

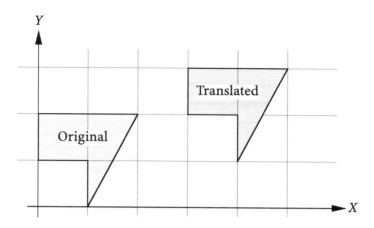

Figure 7.1 *The translated shape results by adding 3 to every x-coordinate, and 1 to every y-coordinate of the original shape.*

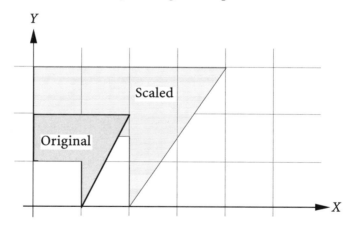

Figure 7.2 *The scaled shape results by multiplying every x-coordinate by 2 and every y-coordinate by 1.5.*

Reflection

To make a reflection of a shape relative to the *y*-axis, we simply reverse the sign of the *x*-coordinate, leaving the *y*-coordinate unchanged

$$x' = -x$$

$$y' = y \qquad\qquad (7.2)$$

and to reflect a shape relative to the x-axis we reverse the y-coordinates:

$$x' = x$$

$$y' = -y \qquad\qquad (7.3)$$

Examples of reflections are shown in Figure 7.3.

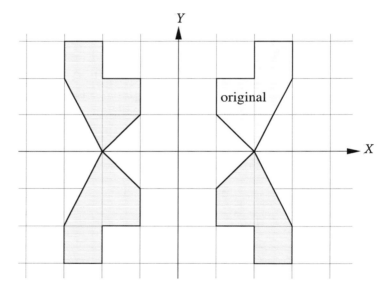

Figure 7.3 *The top right-hand shape can give rise to the three reflections simply by reversing the signs of coordinates.*

Before proceeding, we pause to introduce matrix notation so that we can develop further transformations using algebra and matrices simultaneously.

Matrices

Matrix notation was investigated by the British mathematician Arthur Cayley around 1858. Caley formalized matrix algebra, along with the American mathematicians Benjamin and Charles Pierce. Also, by the start of the 19th century Carl Gauss (1777–1855) had proved that transformations were not commutative, i.e. $T_1 \times T_2 \neq T_2 \times T_1$, and Caley's matrix notation would clarify such observations. For example, consider the transformation T_1:

$$T_1 \qquad \begin{aligned} x' &= ax + by \\ y' &= cx + dy \end{aligned} \tag{7.4}$$

and another transformation T_2 that transforms T_1:

$$T_2 \times T_1 \qquad \begin{aligned} x'' &= Ax' + By' \\ y'' &= Cx' + Dy' \end{aligned} \tag{7.5}$$

If we substitute the full definition of T_1 we get

$$T_2 \times T_1 \qquad \begin{aligned} x'' &= A(ax + by) + B(cx + dy) \\ y'' &= C(ax + by) + D(cx + dy) \end{aligned} \tag{7.6}$$

which simplifies to

$$T_2 \times T_1 \qquad \begin{aligned} x'' &= (Aa + Bc)x + (Ab + Bd)y \\ y'' &= (Ca + Dc)x + (Cb + Dd)y \end{aligned} \tag{7.7}$$

Caley proposed separating the constants from the variables, as follows:

$$T_1 \qquad \begin{bmatrix} x' \\ y' \end{bmatrix} = \begin{bmatrix} a & b \\ c & d \end{bmatrix} \cdot \begin{bmatrix} x \\ y \end{bmatrix} \tag{7.8}$$

where the square matrix of constants in the middle determines the transformation. The algebraic form is recreated by taking the top variable x', introducing the $=$ sign, and multiplying the top row of constants $[a \ b]$ individually by the last column vector containing x and y. We then examine the second variable y', introduce the $=$ sign, and multiply the bottom row of constants $[c \ d]$ individually by the last *column* vector containing x and y, to create

$$x' = ax + by$$

$$y' = cx + dy \tag{7.9}$$

Using Caley's notation, the product $T_2 \times T_1$ is

$$\begin{bmatrix} x'' \\ y'' \end{bmatrix} = \begin{bmatrix} A & B \\ C & D \end{bmatrix} \cdot \begin{bmatrix} x' \\ y' \end{bmatrix} \qquad (7.10)$$

But the notation also intimated that

$$\begin{bmatrix} x'' \\ y'' \end{bmatrix} = \begin{bmatrix} A & B \\ C & D \end{bmatrix} \cdot \begin{bmatrix} a & b \\ c & d \end{bmatrix} \cdot \begin{bmatrix} x \\ y \end{bmatrix} \qquad (7.11)$$

and when we multiply the two *inner matrices* together they must produce

$$x'' = (Aa + Bc)x + (Ab + Bd)y$$

$$y'' = (Ca + Dc)x + (Cb + Dd)y \qquad (7.12)$$

or in matrix form

$$\begin{bmatrix} x'' \\ y'' \end{bmatrix} = \begin{bmatrix} Aa + Bc & Ab + Bd \\ Ca + Dc & Cb + Dd \end{bmatrix} \cdot \begin{bmatrix} x \\ y \end{bmatrix} \qquad (7.13)$$

otherwise the two systems of notation will be inconsistent. This implies that

$$\begin{bmatrix} Aa + Bc & Ab + Bd \\ Ca + Dc & Cb + Dd \end{bmatrix} = \begin{bmatrix} A & B \\ C & D \end{bmatrix} \cdot \begin{bmatrix} a & b \\ c & d \end{bmatrix} \qquad (7.14)$$

which demonstrates how matrices must be multiplied. Here are the rules for matrix multiplication:

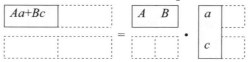

1 The top left-hand corner element $Aa + Bc$ is the product of the top row of the first matrix by the left column of the second matrix.

2 The top right-hand element $Ab + Bd$ is the product of the top row of the first matrix by the right column of the second matrix.

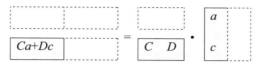

3 The bottom left-hand element *Ca + Dc* is the product of the bottom row of the first matrix by the left column of the second matrix.

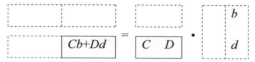

4 The bottom right-hand element *Cb + Dd* is the product of the bottom row of the first matrix by the right column of the second matrix.

It is now a trivial exercise to confirm Gauss's observation that $T_1 \times T_2 \neq T_2 \times T_1$, because if we reverse the transforms $T_2 \times T_1$ to $T_1 \times T_2$ we get

$$\begin{bmatrix} Aa + Bc & Ab + Bd \\ Ca + Dc & Cb + Dd \end{bmatrix} = \begin{bmatrix} a & b \\ c & d \end{bmatrix} \cdot \begin{bmatrix} A & B \\ C & D \end{bmatrix} \qquad (7.15)$$

which shows conclusively that the product of two transforms is not commutative.

One immediate problem with this notation is that there is no apparent mechanism to add or subtract a constant such as *c* or *f*:

$$x' = ax + by + c$$

$$y' = dx + ey + f \qquad (7.16)$$

Mathematicians resolved this in the 19th century, by the use of *homogeneous coordinates*. But before we look at this idea, it must be pointed out that currently there are two systems of matrix notation in use.

Systems of notation

Over the years, two systems of matrix notation have evolved: one where the matrix multiplies a column vector, as described above, and another where a *row vector* multiplies the matrix:

$$[x' \quad y'] = [x \quad y] \cdot \begin{bmatrix} a & c \\ b & d \end{bmatrix} \tag{7.17}$$

Note how the elements of the matrix are transposed to accommodate the algebraic correctness of the transformation. There is no preferred system of notation, and you will find technical books and papers supporting both. For example, *Computer Graphics: Principles and Practice* (Foley *et al.*, 1990) employs the column vector notation, whereas the *Gems* books (Glassner *et al.*, 1990) employ the row vector notation. The important thing to remember is that the rows and columns of the matrix are transposed when moving between the two systems. When we refer to a row vector in this book it will have a superscript ^{T}, e.g. $[x\ y\ z]^T$.

The determinant of a matrix

The *determinant* of a 2×2 matrix is a scalar quantity computed. Given a matrix

$\begin{bmatrix} a & b \\ c & d \end{bmatrix}$ its determinant is $ad - cb$ and is represented by

$$\begin{vmatrix} a & b \\ c & d \end{vmatrix} \tag{7.18}$$

For example, the determinant of

$\begin{bmatrix} 3 & 2 \\ 1 & 2 \end{bmatrix}$ is $3 \times 2 - 1 \times 2 = 4$

Later, we will discover that the determinant of a 2×2 matrix determines the change in area that occurs when a polygon is transformed by the matrix. For example, if the determinant is 1, there is no change in area, but if the determinant is 2, the polygon's area is doubled.

Homogeneous coordinates

Homogeneous coordinates surfaced in the early 19th century, when they were independently proposed by Möbius (who also invented a one-sided curled band, the Möbius strip), Feuerbach, Bobillier, and Plücker. Möbius named them *barycentric coordinates*. They have also been called *areal coordinates* because of their area-calculating properties.

Basically, homogeneous coordinates define a point in a plane using three coordinates instead of two. Initially, Plücker located a homogeneous point relative to the sides of a triangle, but later revised his notation to the one employed in contemporary mathematics and computer graphics. This states that for a point P with coordinates (x, y) there exists a homogeneous point (x, y, t) such that $X = x/t$ and $Y = y/t$. For example, the point $(3, 4)$ has homogeneous coordinates $(6, 8, 2)$, because $3 = 6/2$ and $4 = 8/2$. But the homogeneous point $(6, 8, 2)$ is not unique to $(3, 4)$; $(12, 16, 4)$, $(15, 20, 5)$ and $(300, 400, 100)$ are all possible homogeneous coordinates for $(3, 4)$.

The reason why this coordinate system is called 'homogeneous' is because it is possible to transform functions such as $f(x, y)$ into the form $f(x/t, y/t)$ without disturbing the degree of the curve. To the non-mathematician this may not seem anything to get excited about, but in the field of projective geometry it is a very powerful concept.

For our purposes, we can imagine that a collection of homogeneous points of the form (x, y, t) exist on an xy-plane where t is the z-coordinate, as illustrated in Figure 7.4. The figure shows a triangle on the $t = 1$ plane, and a similar triangle, much larger, on a more distant plane. Thus instead of working in two dimensions, we can work on an arbitrary xy-plane in three dimensions. The t- or z-coordinate of the plane is immaterial because the x- and y-coordinates are eventually scaled by t. However, to keep things simple it seems a good idea to choose $t = 1$. This means that the point (x, y) has homogeneous coordinates $(x, y, 1)$, making scaling unnecessary.

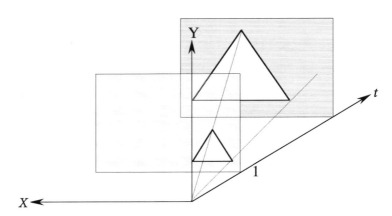

Figure 7.4 *2D homogeneous coordinates can be visualized as a plane in 3D space, generally where t = 1, for convenience.*

If we substitute 3D homogeneous coordinates for traditional 2D Cartesian coordinates, we must attach a 1 to every (x, y) pair. When a point $(x, y, 1)$ is transformed, it will emerge as $(x', y', 1)$, and we discard the 1. This may seem a futile exercise, but it resolves the problem of creating a translation transformation.

Consider the following transformation on the homogeneous point $(x, y, 1)$:

$$\begin{bmatrix} x' \\ y' \\ 1 \end{bmatrix} = \begin{bmatrix} a & b & c \\ d & e & f \\ 0 & 0 & 1 \end{bmatrix} \cdot \begin{bmatrix} x \\ y \\ 1 \end{bmatrix} \qquad (7.19)$$

This expands to

$$x' = ax + by + c$$
$$y' = dx + ey + f$$
$$1 = 1 \qquad (7.20)$$

which solves the above problem of adding a constant.

Let's now go on to see how homogeneous coordinates are used in practice.

2D translation

The algebraic and matrix notation for 2D translation is

$$x' = x + t_x$$
$$y' = y + t_y \tag{7.21}$$

or, using matrices,

$$\begin{bmatrix} x' \\ y' \\ 1 \end{bmatrix} = \begin{bmatrix} 1 & 0 & t_x \\ 0 & 1 & t_y \\ 0 & 0 & 1 \end{bmatrix} \cdot \begin{bmatrix} x \\ y \\ 1 \end{bmatrix} \tag{7.22}$$

2D scaling

The algebraic and matrix notation for 2D scaling is

$$x' = s_x x$$
$$y' = s_y y \tag{7.23}$$

or, using matrices,

$$\begin{bmatrix} x' \\ y' \\ 1 \end{bmatrix} = \begin{bmatrix} s_x & 0 & 0 \\ 0 & s_y & 0 \\ 0 & 0 & 1 \end{bmatrix} \cdot \begin{bmatrix} x \\ y \\ 1 \end{bmatrix} \tag{7.24}$$

The scaling action is relative to the origin, i.e. the point $(0,0)$ remains $(0,0)$ All other points move away from the origin. To scale relative to another point (p_x, p_y) we first subtract (p_x, p_y) from (x, y) respectively. This effectively translates the reference point (p_x, p_y) back to the origin. Second, we perform the scaling operation, and third, add (p_x, p_y) back to (x, y) respectively, to compensate for the original subtraction. Algebraically this is

$$x' = s_x(x - p_x) + p_x$$
$$y' = s_y(y - p_y) + p_y \tag{7.25}$$

which simplifies to

$$x' = s_x x + p_x(1 - s_x)$$

$$y' = s_y y + p_y(1 - s_y) \tag{7.26}$$

or in a homogeneous matrix form

$$\begin{bmatrix} x' \\ y' \\ 1 \end{bmatrix} = \begin{bmatrix} s_x & 0 & p_x(1 - s_x) \\ 0 & s_y & p_y(1 - s_y) \\ 0 & 0 & 1 \end{bmatrix} \cdot \begin{bmatrix} x \\ y \\ 1 \end{bmatrix} \tag{7.27}$$

For example, to scale a shape by 2 relative to the point $(1, 1)$ the matrix is

$$\begin{bmatrix} x' \\ y' \\ 1 \end{bmatrix} = \begin{bmatrix} 2 & 0 & -1 \\ 0 & 2 & -1 \\ 0 & 0 & 1 \end{bmatrix} \cdot \begin{bmatrix} x \\ y \\ 1 \end{bmatrix}$$

2D reflections

The matrix notation for reflecting about the y-axis is:

$$\begin{bmatrix} x' \\ y' \\ 1 \end{bmatrix} = \begin{bmatrix} -1 & 0 & 0 \\ 0 & 1 & 0 \\ 0 & 0 & 1 \end{bmatrix} \cdot \begin{bmatrix} x \\ y \\ 1 \end{bmatrix} \tag{7.28}$$

or about the x-axis

$$\begin{bmatrix} x' \\ y' \\ 1 \end{bmatrix} = \begin{bmatrix} 1 & 0 & 0 \\ 0 & -1 & 0 \\ 0 & 0 & 1 \end{bmatrix} \cdot \begin{bmatrix} x \\ y \\ 1 \end{bmatrix} \tag{7.29}$$

However, to make a reflection about an arbitrary vertical or horizontal axis we need to introduce some more algebraic deception. For example, to make a reflection about the vertical axis $x = 1$, we first subtract 1 from the x-coordinate. This effectively makes the $x = 1$ axis coincident with the major y-axis. Next we perform the reflection by reversing the sign of the modified x-coordinate. And finally, we add 1 to the reflected coordinate to compensate for the original subtraction. Algebraically, the three steps are

$x_1 = x - 1$

$x_2 = -(x - 1)$

$x' = -(x - 1) + 1$

which simplifies to

$x' = -x + 2$

$y' = y$ (7.30)

or in matrix form,

$$\begin{bmatrix} x' \\ y' \\ 1 \end{bmatrix} = \begin{bmatrix} -1 & 0 & 2 \\ 0 & 1 & 0 \\ 0 & 0 & 1 \end{bmatrix} \cdot \begin{bmatrix} x \\ y \\ 1 \end{bmatrix}$$ (7.31)

Figure 7.5 illustrates this process.

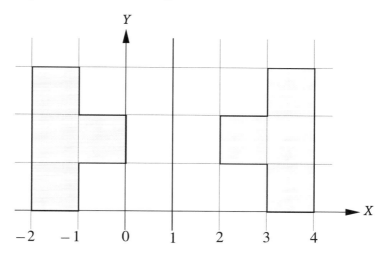

Figure 7.5 *The shape on the right is reflected about the x = 1 axis.*

In general, to reflect a shape about an arbitrary y-axis, $y = a_x$, the following transform is required:

$x' = -(x - a_x) + a_x \qquad = -x + 2a_x$

$y' = y$ (7.32)

or, in matrix form,

$$\begin{bmatrix} x' \\ y' \\ 1 \end{bmatrix} = \begin{bmatrix} -1 & 0 & 2a_x \\ 0 & 1 & 0 \\ 0 & 0 & 1 \end{bmatrix} \cdot \begin{bmatrix} x \\ y \\ 1 \end{bmatrix} \tag{7.33}$$

Similarly, this transform is used for reflections about an arbitrary x-axis, $y = a_y$:

$$x' = x$$

$$y' = -(y - a_y) + a_y = -y + 2a_y \tag{7.34}$$

or, in matrix form,

$$\begin{bmatrix} x' \\ y' \\ 1 \end{bmatrix} = \begin{bmatrix} 1 & 0 & 0 \\ 0 & -1 & 2a_y \\ 0 & 0 & 1 \end{bmatrix} \cdot \begin{bmatrix} x \\ y \\ 1 \end{bmatrix} \tag{7.35}$$

2D shearing

A shape is sheared by leaning it over at an angle β. Figure 7.6 illustrates the geometry, and we see that the y-coordinate remains unchanged but the x-coordinate is a function of y and $\tan(\beta)$.

$$x' = x + y \tan(\beta)$$

$$y' = y \tag{7.36}$$

or, in matrix form,

$$\begin{bmatrix} x' \\ y' \\ 1 \end{bmatrix} = \begin{bmatrix} 1 & \tan(\beta) & 0 \\ 0 & 1 & 0 \\ 0 & 0 & 1 \end{bmatrix} \cdot \begin{bmatrix} x \\ y \\ 1 \end{bmatrix} \tag{7.37}$$

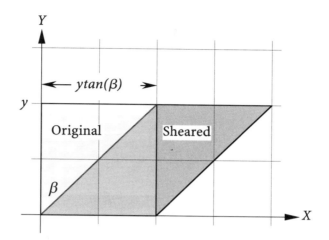

Figure 7.6 *The original square shape is sheared to the right by an angle β, and the horizontal shift is proportional to ytan(β)*

2D rotation

Figure 7.7 shows a point $P(x, y)$ which is to be rotated by an angle β about the origin to $P'(x', y')$. It can be seen that

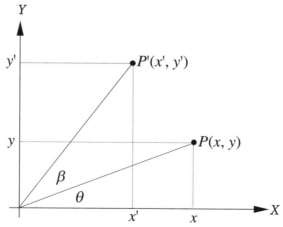

Figure 7.7 *The point $P(x, y)$ is rotated through an angle β to $P'(x', y')$.*

$$x' = R\cos(\theta + \beta)$$
$$y' = R\sin(\theta + \beta) \tag{7.38}$$

therefore

$$x' = R(\cos(\theta)\cos(\beta) - \sin(\theta)\sin(\beta))$$
$$y' = R(\sin(\theta)\cos(\beta) + \cos(\theta)\sin(\beta))$$

$$x' = R\left(\frac{x}{R}\cos(\beta) - \frac{y}{R}\sin(\beta)\right)$$

$$y' = R\left(\frac{y}{R}\cos(\beta) + \frac{x}{R}\sin(\beta)\right)$$

$$x' = x\cos(\beta) - y\sin(\beta)$$
$$y' = x\sin(\beta) + y\cos(\beta) \tag{7.39}$$

or, in matrix form,

$$\begin{bmatrix} x' \\ y' \\ 1 \end{bmatrix} = \begin{bmatrix} \cos(\beta) & -\sin(\beta) & 0 \\ \sin(\beta) & \cos(\beta) & 0 \\ 0 & 0 & 1 \end{bmatrix} \cdot \begin{bmatrix} x \\ y \\ 1 \end{bmatrix} \tag{7.40}$$

For example, to rotate a point by 90° the matrix becomes

$$\begin{bmatrix} x' \\ y' \\ 1 \end{bmatrix} = \begin{bmatrix} 0 & -1 & 0 \\ 1 & 0 & 0 \\ 0 & 0 & 1 \end{bmatrix} \cdot \begin{bmatrix} x \\ y \\ 1 \end{bmatrix}$$

Thus the point $(1, 0)$ becomes $(0, 1)$. If we rotate by 360° the matrix becomes

$$\begin{bmatrix} x' \\ y' \\ 1 \end{bmatrix} = \begin{bmatrix} 1 & 0 & 0 \\ 0 & 1 & 0 \\ 0 & 0 & 1 \end{bmatrix} \cdot \begin{bmatrix} x \\ y \\ 1 \end{bmatrix}$$

Such a matrix has a null effect and is called an *identity matrix*.

To rotate a point (x, y) about an arbitrary point (p_x, p_y) we first subtract (p_x, p_y) from the coordinates (x, y) respectively. This enables us to perform the rotation about the origin. Second, we perform the rotation, and third, we add (p_x, p_y) to compensate for the original subtraction. Here are the steps:

1 Subtract (p_x, p_y):

$$x_1 = (x - p_x)$$

$$y_1 = (y - p_y)$$

2 Rotate β about the origin:

$$x_2 = (x - p_x)\cos(\beta) - (y - p_y)\sin(\beta)$$

$$y_2 = (x - p_x)\sin(\beta) + (y - p_y)\cos(\beta)$$

3 Add (p_x, p_y):

$$x' = (x - p_x)\cos(\beta) - (y - p_y)\sin(\beta) + p_x$$

$$y' = (x - p_x)\sin(\beta) + (y - p_y)\cos(\beta) + p_y$$

Simplifying,

$$x' = x \cos(\beta) - y \sin(\beta) + p_x(1 - \cos(\beta)) + p_y\sin(\beta)$$

$$y' = x \sin(\beta) + y \cos(\beta) + p_y(1 - \cos(\beta)) - p_x\sin(\beta) \quad (7.41)$$

and, in matrix form,

$$\begin{bmatrix} x' \\ y' \\ 1 \end{bmatrix} = \begin{bmatrix} \cos(\beta) & -\sin(\beta) & p_x(1-\cos(\beta))+p_y\sin(\beta) \\ \sin(\beta) & \cos(\beta) & p_y(1-\cos(\beta))-p_x\sin(\beta) \\ 0 & 0 & 1 \end{bmatrix} \cdot \begin{bmatrix} x \\ y \\ 1 \end{bmatrix}$$

$$(7.42)$$

If we now consider rotating a point 90° about the point $(1, 1)$ the matrix operation becomes

$$\begin{bmatrix} x' \\ y' \\ 1 \end{bmatrix} = \begin{bmatrix} 0 & -1 & 2 \\ 1 & 0 & 0 \\ 0 & 0 & 1 \end{bmatrix} \cdot \begin{bmatrix} x \\ y \\ 1 \end{bmatrix}$$

A simple test is to substitute the point $(2, 1)$ for (x, y): it is transformed correctly to $(1, 2)$.

The algebraic approach in deriving the above transforms is relatively easy. However, it is also possible to use matrices to derive compound transformations, such as a reflection relative to an arbitrary line and scaling and rotation relative to an arbitrary point. These transformations are called *affine*, as parallel lines remain parallel after being transformed. One cannot always guarantee that angles and lengths are preserved, as the scaling transformation can alter these when different x and y scaling factors are used. For completeness, we will repeat these transformations from a matrix perspective.

2D scaling

The strategy we used to scale a point (x, y) relative to some arbitrary point (p_x, p_y) was to first, translate $(-p_x, -p_y)$; second, perform the scaling; and third, translate (p_x, p_y). These three transforms can be represented in matrix form as follows:

$$\begin{bmatrix} x' \\ y' \\ 1 \end{bmatrix} = [\text{translate}(p_x, p_y)] \cdot [\text{scale}(s_x, s_y)] \cdot [\text{translate}(-p_x, -p_y)] \cdot \begin{bmatrix} x \\ y \\ 1 \end{bmatrix}$$

which expands to

$$\begin{bmatrix} x' \\ y' \\ 1 \end{bmatrix} = \begin{bmatrix} 1 & 0 & p_x \\ 0 & 1 & p_y \\ 0 & 0 & 1 \end{bmatrix} \cdot \begin{bmatrix} s_x & 0 & 0 \\ 0 & s_y & 0 \\ 0 & 0 & 1 \end{bmatrix} \cdot \begin{bmatrix} 1 & 0 & -p_x \\ 0 & 1 & -p_y \\ 0 & 0 & 1 \end{bmatrix} \cdot \begin{bmatrix} x \\ y \\ 1 \end{bmatrix} \quad (7.43)$$

Note the sequence of the transforms, as this often causes confusion. The first transform acting on the point $(x, y, 1)$ is translate$(-p_x, -p_y)$, followed by scale(s_x, s_y), followed by translate(p_x, p_y). If they are placed in any other sequence, you will discover, like Gauss, that transforms are not commutative!

We can now concatenate these matrices into a single matrix by multiplying them together. This can be done in any sequence, so long as we preserve the original order. Let's start with scale(s_x, s_y) and translate$(-p_x, -p_y)$. This produces

$$\begin{bmatrix} x' \\ y' \\ 1 \end{bmatrix} = \begin{bmatrix} 1 & 0 & p_x \\ 0 & 1 & p_y \\ 0 & 0 & 1 \end{bmatrix} \cdot \begin{bmatrix} s_x & 0 & -s_x p_x \\ 0 & s_y & -s_y p_y \\ 0 & 0 & 1 \end{bmatrix} \cdot \begin{bmatrix} x \\ y \\ 1 \end{bmatrix}$$

and finally

$$\begin{bmatrix} x' \\ y' \\ 1 \end{bmatrix} = \begin{bmatrix} s_x & 0 & p_x(1-s_x) \\ 0 & s_y & p_y(1-s_y) \\ 0 & 0 & 1 \end{bmatrix} \cdot \begin{bmatrix} x \\ y \\ 1 \end{bmatrix} \qquad (7.44)$$

which is the same as the previous transform (7.27).

2D reflections

A reflection about the y-axis is given by

$$\begin{bmatrix} x' \\ y' \\ 1 \end{bmatrix} = \begin{bmatrix} -1 & 0 & 0 \\ 0 & 1 & 0 \\ 0 & 0 & 1 \end{bmatrix} \cdot \begin{bmatrix} x \\ y \\ 1 \end{bmatrix} \qquad (7.45)$$

Therefore, using matrices, we can reason that a reflection transform about an arbitrary axis $x = a_x$, parallel with the y-axis, is given by

$$\begin{bmatrix} x' \\ y' \\ 1 \end{bmatrix} = [\text{translate}(a_x, 0)] \cdot [\text{reflection}] \cdot [\text{translate}(-a_x, 0)] \cdot \begin{bmatrix} x \\ y \\ 1 \end{bmatrix}$$

which expands to

$$\begin{bmatrix} x' \\ y' \\ 1 \end{bmatrix} = \begin{bmatrix} 1 & 0 & a_x \\ 0 & 1 & 0 \\ 0 & 0 & 1 \end{bmatrix} \cdot \begin{bmatrix} -1 & 0 & 0 \\ 0 & 1 & 0 \\ 0 & 0 & 1 \end{bmatrix} \begin{bmatrix} 1 & 0 & -a_x \\ 0 & 1 & 0 \\ 0 & 0 & 1 \end{bmatrix} \cdot \begin{bmatrix} x \\ y \\ 1 \end{bmatrix}$$

We can now concatenate these matrices into a single matrix by multiplying them together. Let's begin by multiplying the reflection and the translate($-a_x$, 0) matrices together. This produces

$$\begin{bmatrix} x' \\ y' \\ 1 \end{bmatrix} = \begin{bmatrix} 1 & 0 & a_x \\ 0 & 1 & 0 \\ 0 & 0 & 1 \end{bmatrix} \cdot \begin{bmatrix} -1 & 0 & a_x \\ 0 & 1 & 0 \\ 0 & 0 & 1 \end{bmatrix} \cdot \begin{bmatrix} x \\ y \\ 1 \end{bmatrix}$$

and finally

$$\begin{bmatrix} x' \\ y' \\ 1 \end{bmatrix} = \begin{bmatrix} -1 & 0 & 2a_x \\ 0 & 1 & 0 \\ 0 & 0 & 1 \end{bmatrix} \cdot \begin{bmatrix} x \\ y \\ 1 \end{bmatrix} \qquad (7.46)$$

which is the same as the previous transform (7.33).

2D rotation about an arbitrary point

A rotation about the origin is given by

$$\begin{bmatrix} x' \\ y' \\ 1 \end{bmatrix} = \begin{bmatrix} \cos(\beta) & -\sin(\beta) & 0 \\ \sin(\beta) & \cos(\beta) & 0 \\ 0 & 0 & 1 \end{bmatrix} \cdot \begin{bmatrix} x \\ y \\ 1 \end{bmatrix} \qquad (7.47)$$

Therefore, using matrices, we can develop a rotation about an arbitrary point (p_x, p_y) as follows:

$$\begin{bmatrix} x' \\ y' \\ 1 \end{bmatrix} = [\text{translate}(p_x, p_y)] \cdot [\text{rotate } \beta] \cdot [\text{translate}(-p_x, -p_y)] \cdot \begin{bmatrix} x \\ y \\ 1 \end{bmatrix}$$

which expands to

$$\begin{bmatrix} x' \\ y' \\ 1 \end{bmatrix} = \begin{bmatrix} 1 & 0 & p_x \\ 0 & 1 & p_y \\ 0 & 0 & 1 \end{bmatrix} \cdot \begin{bmatrix} \cos(\beta) & -\sin(\beta) & 0 \\ \sin(\beta) & \cos(\beta) & 0 \\ 0 & 0 & 1 \end{bmatrix} \cdot \begin{bmatrix} 1 & 0 & -p_x \\ 0 & 1 & -p_y \\ 0 & 0 & 1 \end{bmatrix} \cdot \begin{bmatrix} x \\ y \\ 1 \end{bmatrix}$$

We can now concatenate these matrices into a single matrix by multiplying them together. Let's begin by multiplying the rotateβ and the translate$(-p_x, -p_y)$ matrices together. This produces

$$\begin{bmatrix} x' \\ y' \\ 1 \end{bmatrix} = \begin{bmatrix} 1 & 0 & p_x \\ 0 & 1 & p_y \\ 0 & 0 & 1 \end{bmatrix} \cdot \begin{bmatrix} \cos(\beta) & -\sin(\beta) & -p_x\cos(\beta)+p_y\sin(\beta) \\ \sin(\beta) & \cos(\beta) & -p_x\sin(\beta)-p_y\cos(\beta) \\ 0 & 0 & 1 \end{bmatrix} \begin{bmatrix} x \\ y \\ 1 \end{bmatrix}$$

and finally

$$\begin{bmatrix} x' \\ y' \\ 1 \end{bmatrix} = \begin{bmatrix} \cos(\beta) & -\sin(\beta) & p_x(1-\cos(\beta))+p_y\sin(\beta) \\ \sin(\beta) & \cos(\beta) & p_y(1-\cos(\beta))-p_x\sin(\beta) \\ 0 & 0 & 1 \end{bmatrix} \cdot \begin{bmatrix} x \\ y \\ 1 \end{bmatrix}$$

(7.48)

which is the same as the previous transform (7.42).

I hope it is now is obvious to the reader that one can derive all sorts of transforms either algebraically, or by using matrices – it is just a question of convenience.

3D transformations

Now we come to transformations in three dimensions, where we apply the same reasoning as in two dimensions. Scaling and translation are basically the same, but where in 2D we rotated a shape about a point, in 3D we rotate an object about an axis.

3D translation

The algebra is so simple for 3D translation that we can write the homogeneous matrix directly:

$$\begin{bmatrix} x' \\ y' \\ z' \\ 1 \end{bmatrix} = \begin{bmatrix} 1 & 0 & 0 & t_x \\ 0 & 1 & 0 & t_y \\ 0 & 0 & 1 & t_z \\ 0 & 0 & 0 & 1 \end{bmatrix} \cdot \begin{bmatrix} x \\ y \\ z \\ 1 \end{bmatrix}$$

(7.49)

3D scaling

The algebra for 3D scaling is

$$x' = s_x x$$
$$y' = s_y y$$
$$z' = s_z z \tag{7.50}$$

which in matrix form is

$$\begin{bmatrix} x' \\ y' \\ z' \\ 1 \end{bmatrix} = \begin{bmatrix} s_x & 0 & 0 & 0 \\ 0 & s_y & 0 & 0 \\ 0 & 0 & s_z & 0 \\ 0 & 0 & 0 & 1 \end{bmatrix} \cdot \begin{bmatrix} x \\ y \\ z \\ 1 \end{bmatrix} \tag{7.51}$$

The scaling is relative to the origin, but we can arrange for it to be relative to an arbitrary point (p_x, p_y, p_z) with the following algebra:

$$x' = s_x(x - p_x) + p_x$$
$$y' = s_y(y - p_y) + p_y$$
$$z' = s_z(z - p_2) + p_z \tag{7.52}$$

which in matrix form is

$$\begin{bmatrix} x' \\ y' \\ z' \\ 1 \end{bmatrix} = \begin{bmatrix} s_x & 0 & 0 & p_x(1-s_x) \\ 0 & s_y & 0 & p_y(1-s_y) \\ 0 & 0 & s_z & p_z(1-s_z) \\ 0 & 0 & 0 & 1 \end{bmatrix} \cdot \begin{bmatrix} x \\ y \\ z \\ 1 \end{bmatrix} \tag{7.53}$$

3D rotations

In two dimensions a shape is rotated about a point, whether it be the origin or some arbitrary position. In three dimensions an object is rotated about an axis, whether it be the x-, y- or z-axis, or some arbitrary axis. To begin with, let's look at rotating a vertex about one of the three orthogonal axes; such rotations are called *Euler rotations* after the Swiss mathematician Leonhard Euler (1707–1783).

Recall that a general 2D-rotation transform is given by

$$\begin{bmatrix} x' \\ y' \\ 1 \end{bmatrix} = \begin{bmatrix} \cos(\beta) & -\sin(\beta) & 0 \\ \sin(\beta) & \cos(\beta) & 0 \\ 0 & 0 & 1 \end{bmatrix} \cdot \begin{bmatrix} x \\ y \\ 1 \end{bmatrix} \tag{7.54}$$

which in 3D can be visualized as rotating a point $P(x, y, z)$ on a plane parallel with the *xy*-plane as shown in Figure 7.8. In algebraic terms this can be written as

$$x' = x \cos(\beta) - y \sin(\beta)$$
$$y' = x \sin(\beta) + y \cos(\beta)$$
$$z' = z \tag{7.55}$$

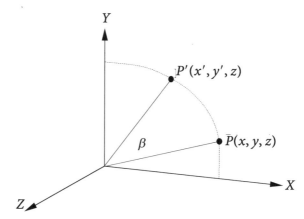

Figure 7.8 *Rotating P about the z-axis.*

Therefore, the 3D transform can be written as

$$\begin{bmatrix} x' \\ y' \\ z' \\ 1 \end{bmatrix} = \begin{bmatrix} \cos(\beta) & -\sin(\beta) & 0 & 0 \\ \sin(\beta) & \cos(\beta) & 0 & 0 \\ 0 & 0 & 1 & 0 \\ 0 & 0 & 0 & 1 \end{bmatrix} \cdot \begin{bmatrix} x \\ y \\ z \\ 1 \end{bmatrix} \tag{7.56}$$

which basically rotates a point about the *z*-axis.

When rotating about the x-axis, the x-coordinate remains constant while the y- and z-coordinates are changed. Algebraically, this is

$$x' = x$$

$$y' = y\cos(\beta) - z\sin(\beta)$$

$$z' = y\sin(\beta) + z\cos(\beta) \tag{7.57}$$

or, in matrix form,

$$
\begin{bmatrix} x' \\ y' \\ z' \\ 1 \end{bmatrix} =
\begin{bmatrix}
1 & 0 & 0 & 0 \\
0 & \cos(\beta) & -\sin(\beta) & 0 \\
0 & \sin(\beta) & \cos(\beta) & 0 \\
0 & 0 & 0 & 1
\end{bmatrix} \cdot
\begin{bmatrix} x \\ y \\ z \\ 1 \end{bmatrix} \tag{7.58}
$$

When rotating about the y-axis, the y-coordinate remains constant while the x- and z-coordinates are changed. Algebraically, this is

$$x' = z\sin(\beta) + x\cos(\beta)$$

$$y' = y$$

$$z' = z\cos(\beta) - x\sin(\beta) \tag{7.59}$$

or, in matrix form,

$$
\begin{bmatrix} x' \\ y' \\ z' \\ 1 \end{bmatrix} =
\begin{bmatrix}
\cos(\beta) & 0 & \sin(\beta) & 0 \\
0 & 1 & 0 & 0 \\
-\sin(\beta) & 0 & \cos(\beta) & 0 \\
0 & 0 & 0 & 1
\end{bmatrix} \cdot
\begin{bmatrix} x \\ y \\ z \\ 1 \end{bmatrix} \tag{7.60}
$$

Note that the matrix terms do not appear to share the symmetry seen in the previous two matrices. Nothing has really gone wrong, it is just the way the axes are paired together to rotate the coordinates.

The above rotations are also known as *yaw*, *pitch* and *roll*. Great care should be taken with these terms when referring to other books and technical papers. Sometimes a left-handed system of axes is used rather than a right-handed set, and the vertical axis may be the y-axis or the z-axis.

Consequently, the matrices representing the rotations can vary greatly. In this text all Cartesian coordinate systems are right-handed, and the vertical axis is always the y-axis.

The roll, pitch and yaw angles can be defined as follows:

- *roll* is the angle of rotation about the z-axis
- *pitch* is the angle of rotation about the x-axis
- *yaw* is the angle of rotation about the y-axis.

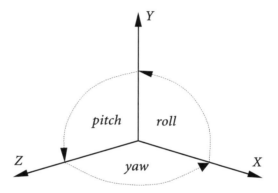

Figure 7.9 *The convention for roll, pitch and yaw angles.*

Figure 7.9 illustrates these rotations and the sign convention. The homogeneous matrices representing these rotations are as follows:

- rotate *roll* about the z-axis:

$$\begin{bmatrix} \cos(roll) & -\sin(roll) & 0 & 0 \\ \sin(roll) & \cos(roll) & 0 & 0 \\ 0 & 0 & 1 & 0 \\ 0 & 0 & 0 & 1 \end{bmatrix} \tag{7.61}$$

- rotate *pitch* about the x-axis:

$$\begin{bmatrix} 1 & 0 & 0 & 0 \\ 0 & \cos(pitch) & -\sin(pitch) & 0 \\ 0 & \sin(pitch) & \cos(pitch) & 0 \\ 0 & 0 & 0 & 1 \end{bmatrix} \tag{7.62}$$

- rotate *yaw* about the *y*-axis:

$$\begin{bmatrix} \cos(yaw) & 0 & \sin(yaw) & 0 \\ 0 & 1 & 0 & 0 \\ -\sin(yaw) & 0 & \cos(yaw) & 0 \\ 0 & 0 & 0 & 1 \end{bmatrix} \tag{7.63}$$

A common sequence for applying these rotations is *roll, pitch, yaw*, as seen in the following transform:

$$\begin{bmatrix} x' \\ y' \\ z' \\ 1 \end{bmatrix} = [yaw] \cdot [pitch] \cdot [roll] \cdot \begin{bmatrix} x \\ y \\ z \\ 1 \end{bmatrix} \tag{7.64}$$

and if a translation is involved,

$$\begin{bmatrix} x' \\ y' \\ z' \\ 1 \end{bmatrix} = [translate] \cdot [yaw] \cdot [pitch] \cdot [roll] \cdot \begin{bmatrix} x \\ y \\ z \\ 1 \end{bmatrix} \tag{7.65}$$

When these rotation transforms are applied, the vertex is first rotated about the *z*-axis (roll), followed by a rotation about the *x*-axis (pitch), followed by a rotation about the *y*-axis (yaw). Euler rotations are relative to the fixed frame of reference. This is not always easy to visualize, as one's attention is normally with the rotating frame of reference. Let's consider a simple example where an axial system is subjected to a pitch rotation followed by a yaw rotation relative to fixed frame of reference.

We begin with two frames of reference *XYZ* and *X'Y'Z'* mutually aligned. Figure 7.10 shows the orientation of *X'Y'Z'* after it is subjected to a pitch of 90° about the *x*-axis. Figure 7.11 shows the final orientation after *X'Y'Z'* is subjected to a yaw of 90° about the *y*-axis.

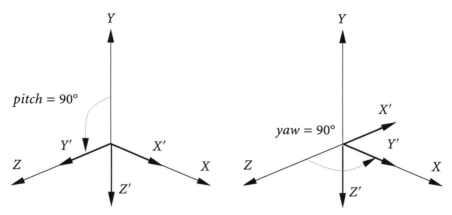

Figure 7.10 *The X′Y′Z′ axial system after a pitch of 90°*

Figure 7.11 *The X′Y′Z′ axial system after a yaw of 90°*

Gimbal lock

Let's take another example starting from the point where the two axial systems are mutually aligned. Figure 7.12 shows the orientation of $X′Y′Z′$ after it is subjected to a roll of 45° about the z-axis, and Figure 7.13 shows the orientation of $X′Y′Z′$ after it is subjected to a pitch of 90° about the x-axis. Now the interesting thing about this orientation is that if we now performed a yaw of 45° about the z-axis, it would rotate the x′-axis towards the x-axis, counteracting the effect of the original roll. Effectively, a yaw has become a negative roll rotation, caused by the 90° pitch. This situation is known as *gimbal lock*, because one degree of rotational freedom has been lost. Quite innocently, we have stumbled across one of the major weaknesses of Euler angles: under certain conditions it is only possible to rotate an object about two axes. One way of preventing this is to create a secondary set of axes constructed from three orthogonal vectors that are also rotated alongside an object or virtual camera. But instead of making the rotations relative to the fixed frame of reference, the roll, pitch and yaw rotations are relative to the rotating frame of reference. Another method is to use quaternions, which will be investigated later in this chapter.

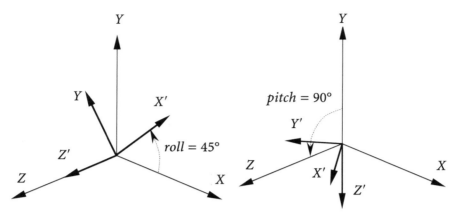

Figure 7.12 *The X′Y′Z′ axial system after a roll of 45°*

Figure 7.13 *The X′Y′Z′ axial system after a pitch of 90°*

Rotating about an axis

The above rotations were relative to the x-, y- and z-axes. Now let's consider rotations about an axis parallel to one of these axes. To begin with, we will rotate about an axis parallel with the z-axis, as shown in Figure 7.14. The scenario is very reminiscent of the 2D case for rotating a point about an arbitrary point, and the general transform is given by

$$\begin{bmatrix} x' \\ y' \\ z' \\ 1 \end{bmatrix} = [translate(p_x, p_y, 0)].[rotate\beta].[translate(-p_x, -p_y, 0)]. \begin{bmatrix} x \\ y \\ z \\ 1 \end{bmatrix}$$

(7.66)

and the matrix is

$$\begin{bmatrix} x' \\ y' \\ z' \\ 1 \end{bmatrix} = \begin{bmatrix} \cos(\beta) & -\sin(\beta) & 0 & p_x(1-\cos(\beta))+p_y\sin(\beta) \\ \sin(\beta) & \cos(\beta) & 0 & p_y(1-\cos(\beta))-p_x\sin(\beta) \\ 0 & 0 & 1 & 0 \\ 0 & 0 & 0 & 1 \end{bmatrix}. \begin{bmatrix} x \\ y \\ z \\ 1 \end{bmatrix}$$

(7.67)

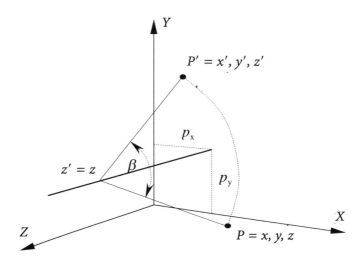

Figure 7.14 *Rotating a point about an axis parallel with the z-axis*

I hope you can see the similarity between rotating in 3D and 2D: the *x*- and *y*-coordinates are updated while the *z*-coordinate is held constant. We can now state the other two matrices for rotating about an axis parallel with the *x*-axis and parallel with the *y*-axis:

• rotating about an axis parallel with the *x*-axis:

$$
\begin{bmatrix} x' \\ y' \\ z' \\ 1 \end{bmatrix} = \begin{bmatrix} 1 & 0 & 0 & 0 \\ 0 & \cos(\beta) & -\sin(\beta) & p_y(1-\cos(\beta))+p_z\sin(\beta) \\ 0 & \sin(\beta) & \cos(\beta) & p_z(1-\cos(\beta))-p_y\sin(\beta) \\ 0 & 0 & 0 & 1 \end{bmatrix} \cdot \begin{bmatrix} x \\ y \\ z \\ 1 \end{bmatrix}
$$

(7.68)

• rotating about an axis parallel with the *y*-axis:

$$
\begin{bmatrix} x' \\ y' \\ z' \\ 1 \end{bmatrix} = \begin{bmatrix} \cos(\beta) & 0 & \sin(\beta) & p_x(1-\cos(\beta))-p_z\sin(\beta) \\ 0 & 1 & 0 & 0 \\ -\sin(\beta) & 0 & \cos(\beta) & p_z(1-\cos(\beta))+p_x\sin(\beta) \\ 0 & 0 & 0 & 1 \end{bmatrix} \cdot \begin{bmatrix} x \\ y \\ z \\ 1 \end{bmatrix}
$$

(7.69)

3D reflections

Reflections in 3D occur with respect to a plane, rather than an axis. The matrix giving the reflection relative to the yz-plane is

$$\begin{bmatrix} x' \\ y' \\ z' \\ 1 \end{bmatrix} = \begin{bmatrix} -1 & 0 & 0 & 0 \\ 0 & 1 & 0 & 0 \\ 0 & 0 & 1 & 0 \\ 0 & 0 & 0 & 1 \end{bmatrix} \cdot \begin{bmatrix} x \\ y \\ z \\ 1 \end{bmatrix} \tag{7.70}$$

and the reflection relative to a plane parallel to, and a_x units from, the yz-plane is

$$\begin{bmatrix} x' \\ y' \\ z' \\ 1 \end{bmatrix} = \begin{bmatrix} -1 & 0 & 0 & 2a_x \\ 0 & 1 & 0 & 0 \\ 0 & 0 & 1 & 0 \\ 0 & 0 & 0 & 1 \end{bmatrix} \cdot \begin{bmatrix} x \\ y \\ z \\ 1 \end{bmatrix} \tag{7.71}$$

It is left to the reader to develop similar matrices for the other major axial planes.

Change of axes

Points in one coordinate system often have to be referenced in another one. For example, to view a 3D scene from an arbitrary position, a virtual camera is positioned in the world space using a series of transformations. An object's coordinates, which are relative to the world frame of reference, are computed relative to the camera's axial system, and then used to develop a perspective projection. Before explaining how this is achieved in 3D, let's examine the simple case of changing axial systems in two dimensions.

2D change of axes

Figure 7.15 shows a point $P(x, y)$ relative to the XY-axes, but we require to know the coordinates relative to the $X'Y'$-axes. To do this, we need to know the relationship between the two coordinate systems, and ideally we want to apply a technique that works in 2D and 3D. If the second coordinate system is a simple translation (t_x, t_y) relative to the reference system, as shown in Figure 7.15, the point $P(x, y)$ has coordinates relative to the translated system $(x - t_x, y - t_y)$:

$$\begin{bmatrix} x' \\ y' \\ 1 \end{bmatrix} = \begin{bmatrix} 1 & 0 & -t_x \\ 0 & 1 & -t_y \\ 0 & 0 & 1 \end{bmatrix} \cdot \begin{bmatrix} x \\ y \\ 1 \end{bmatrix} \tag{7.72}$$

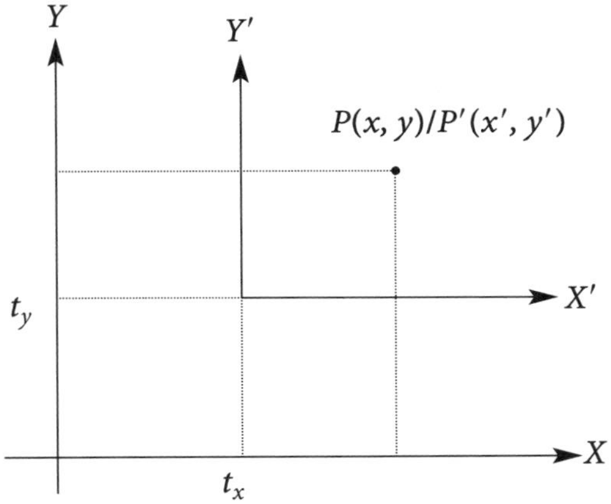

Figure 7.15 *The $X'Y'$-axes are translated by (t_x, t_y).*

If the $X'Y'$-axes are rotated β relative to the XY-axes, as shown in Figure 7.16, a point $P(x, y)$ relative to the XY-axes has coordinates (x', y') relative to the rotated axes given by

$$\begin{bmatrix} x' \\ y' \\ 1 \end{bmatrix} = \begin{bmatrix} \cos(-\beta) & -\sin(-\beta) & 0 \\ \sin(-\beta) & \cos(-\beta) & 0 \\ 0 & 0 & 1 \end{bmatrix} \cdot \begin{bmatrix} x \\ y \\ 1 \end{bmatrix}$$

which simplifies to

$$\begin{bmatrix} x' \\ y' \\ 1 \end{bmatrix} = \begin{bmatrix} \cos(\beta) & \sin(\beta) & 0 \\ -\sin(\beta) & \cos(\beta) & 0 \\ 0 & 0 & 1 \end{bmatrix} \cdot \begin{bmatrix} x \\ y \\ 1 \end{bmatrix} \qquad (7.73)$$

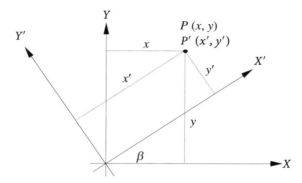

Figure 7.16 *The secondary set of axes are rotated by β.*

When a coordinate system is rotated and translated relative to the reference system, a point $P(x,y)$ has coordinates (x',y') relative to the new axes given by

$$\begin{bmatrix} x' \\ y' \\ 1 \end{bmatrix} = \begin{bmatrix} \cos(\beta) & \sin(\beta) & 0 \\ -\sin(\beta) & \cos(\beta) & 0 \\ 0 & 0 & 1 \end{bmatrix} \cdot \begin{bmatrix} 1 & 0 & -t_x \\ 0 & 1 & -t_y \\ 0 & 0 & 1 \end{bmatrix} \cdot \begin{bmatrix} x \\ y \\ 1 \end{bmatrix}$$

which simplifies to

$$\begin{bmatrix} x' \\ y' \\ 1 \end{bmatrix} = \begin{bmatrix} \cos(\beta) & \sin(\beta) & -t_x\cos(\beta)-t_y\sin(\beta) \\ -\sin(\beta) & \cos(\beta) & t_x\sin(\beta)-t_y\cos(\beta) \\ 0 & 0 & 1 \end{bmatrix} \cdot \begin{bmatrix} x \\ y \\ 1 \end{bmatrix} \quad (7.74)$$

Direction cosines

Direction cosines are the cosines of the angles between a vector and the axes, and for unit vectors they are the vector's components.

Figure 7.17 shows two unit vectors X' and Y', and by inspection the direction cosines for X' are $\cos(\beta)$ and $\cos(90° - \beta)$, which can be rewritten as $\cos(\beta)$ and $\sin(\beta)$, and the direction cosines for Y' are $\cos(90° + \beta)$ and $\cos(\beta)$, which can be rewritten as $-\sin(\beta)$ and $\cos(\beta)$. But these direction cosines $\cos(\beta)$, $\sin(\beta)$, $-\sin(\beta)$ and $\cos(\beta)$ are the four elements of the rotation matrix used above:

$$\begin{bmatrix} \cos(\beta) & \sin(\beta) \\ -\sin(\beta) & \cos(\beta) \end{bmatrix} \tag{7.75}$$

The top row contains the direction cosines for the X'-axis and the bottom row contains the direction cosines for the Y'-axis. This relationship also holds in 3D.

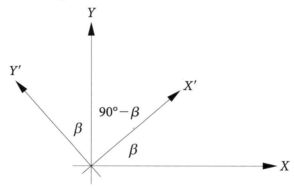

Figure 7.17 *If the X'- and Y'-axes are assumed to be unit vectors their direction cosines form the elements of the rotation matrix.*

Before exploring changes of axes in 3D let's evaluate a simple example in 2D where a set of axes is rotated 45° as shown in Figure 7.18. The appropriate transform is

$$\begin{bmatrix} x' \\ y' \\ 1 \end{bmatrix} = \begin{bmatrix} \cos(45°) & \sin(45°) & 0 \\ -\sin(45°) & \cos(45°) & 0 \\ 0 & 0 & 1 \end{bmatrix} \cdot \begin{bmatrix} x \\ y \\ 1 \end{bmatrix}$$

$$= \begin{bmatrix} 0.707 & 0.707 & 0 \\ -0.707 & 0.707 & 0 \\ 0 & 0 & 1 \end{bmatrix} \cdot \begin{bmatrix} x \\ y \\ 1 \end{bmatrix}$$

The four vertices on a unit square become

$(0, 0) \rightarrow (0, 0)$

$(1, 0) \rightarrow (0.707, -0.707)$

$(1, 1) \rightarrow (1.414, 0)$

$(0, 1) \rightarrow (0.707, 0.707)$

which inspection of Figure 7.18 shows to be correct.

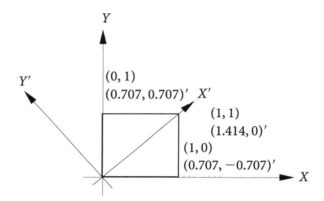

Fig 7.18 *The vertices of a unit square relative to the two axial systems.*

Positioning the virtual camera

Four coordinate systems are used in the computer graphics pipeline: *object space*, *world space*, *camera space* and *image space*.

- The *object space* is a domain where objects are modelled and assembled.
- The *world space* is where objects are positioned and animated through appropriate transforms. The world space also hosts a virtual camera or observer.
- The *camera space* is a transform of the world space to the camera's point of view.

• Finally, *the image space* is a projection – normally perspective – of the camera space onto an image plane.

The transforms considered so far are used to manipulate and position objects within the world space. What we will consider next is how a virtual camera or observer is positioned in world space, and the process of converting world coordinates to camera coordinates. The procedure used generally depends on the method employed to define the camera's frame of reference within the world space, which may involve the use of direction cosines, Euler angles or quaternions. We will examine how each of these techniques could be implemented.

Direction cosines

A 3D unit vector has three components $[x\ y\ z]^T$, which are equal to the cosines of the angles formed between the vector and the three orthogonal axes. These angles are known as *direction cosines* and can be computed taking the dot product of the vector and the Cartesian unit vectors. Figure 7.19 shows the direction cosines and the angles. These direction cosines enable any point $P(x, y, z)$ in one frame of reference to be transformed into $P'(x', y', z')$ in another frame of reference as follows:

$$\begin{bmatrix} x' \\ y' \\ z' \\ 1 \end{bmatrix} = \begin{bmatrix} r_{11} & r_{12} & r_{13} & 0 \\ r_{21} & r_{22} & r_{23} & 0 \\ r_{31} & r_{32} & r_{33} & 0 \\ 0 & 0 & 0 & 1 \end{bmatrix} \cdot \begin{bmatrix} x \\ y \\ z \\ 1 \end{bmatrix} \tag{7.76}$$

where:

r_{11}, r_{12}, r_{13} are the direction cosines of the secondary x-axis

r_{21}, r_{22}, r_{23} are the direction cosines of the secondary y-axis

r_{31}, r_{32}, r_{33} are the direction cosines of the secondary z-axis.

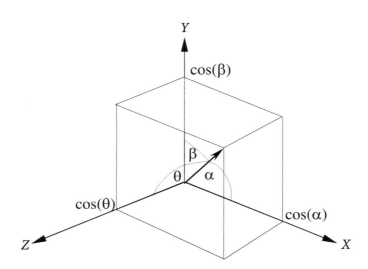

Figure 7.19 *The components of a unit vector are equal to the cosines of the angles between the vector and the axes.*

To illustrate this operation, consider the situation shown in Figure 7.20 which shows two axial systems mutually aligned. Evaluating the direction cosines results in the following matrix transformation:

$$\begin{bmatrix} x' \\ y' \\ z' \\ 1 \end{bmatrix} = \begin{bmatrix} 1 & 0 & 0 & 0 \\ 0 & 1 & 0 & 0 \\ 0 & 0 & 1 & 0 \\ 0 & 0 & 0 & 1 \end{bmatrix} \cdot \begin{bmatrix} x \\ y \\ z \\ 1 \end{bmatrix}$$

which is the identity matrix and implies that $(x', y', z') = (x, y, z)$.

Figure 7.21 shows another situation, and the associated transform is

$$\begin{bmatrix} x' \\ y' \\ z' \\ 1 \end{bmatrix} = \begin{bmatrix} 0 & 1 & 0 & 0 \\ -1 & 0 & 0 & 0 \\ 0 & 0 & 1 & 0 \\ 0 & 0 & 0 & 1 \end{bmatrix} \cdot \begin{bmatrix} x \\ y \\ z \\ 1 \end{bmatrix}$$

Substituting the $(1, 1, 0)$ for (x, y, z) produces values of $(1, -1, 0)$ for (x', y', z') in the new frame of reference, which by inspection is correct.

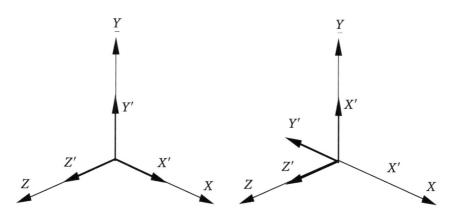

Figure 7.20 *Two axial systems mutually aligned.*

Figure 7.21 *The X' Y' Z' axial system after a roll of 90°.*

If the virtual camera is offset by (t_x, t_y, t_z) the transform relating points in world space to camera space can be expressed as a compound operation consisting of a translation back to the origin, followed by a change of axial systems. This can be expressed as

$$
\begin{bmatrix} x' \\ y' \\ z' \\ 1 \end{bmatrix} = \begin{bmatrix} r_{11} & r_{12} & r_{13} & 0 \\ r_{21} & r_{22} & r_{23} & 0 \\ r_{31} & r_{32} & r_{33} & 0 \\ 0 & 0 & 0 & 1 \end{bmatrix} \cdot \begin{bmatrix} 1 & 0 & 0 & -t_x \\ 0 & 1 & 0 & -t_y \\ 0 & 0 & 1 & -t_z \\ 0 & 0 & 0 & 1 \end{bmatrix} \cdot \begin{bmatrix} x \\ y \\ z \\ 1 \end{bmatrix} \tag{7.77}
$$

As an example, consider the situation shown in Figure 7.22. The values of (t_x, t_y, t_z) are $(10, 1, 1)$, and the direction cosines are as shown in the following matrix operation:

$$
\begin{bmatrix} x' \\ y' \\ z' \\ 1 \end{bmatrix} = \begin{bmatrix} -1 & 0 & 0 & 0 \\ 0 & 1 & 0 & 0 \\ 0 & 0 & -1 & 0 \\ 0 & 0 & 0 & 1 \end{bmatrix} \cdot \begin{bmatrix} 1 & 0 & 0 & -10 \\ 0 & 1 & 0 & -1 \\ 0 & 0 & 1 & -1 \\ 0 & 0 & 0 & 1 \end{bmatrix} \cdot \begin{bmatrix} x \\ y \\ z \\ 1 \end{bmatrix}
$$

which concatenates to

$$
\begin{bmatrix} x' \\ y' \\ z' \\ 1 \end{bmatrix} = \begin{bmatrix} -1 & 0 & 0 & 10 \\ 0 & 1 & 0 & -1 \\ 0 & 0 & -1 & 1 \\ 0 & 0 & 0 & 1 \end{bmatrix} \cdot \begin{bmatrix} x \\ y \\ z \\ 1 \end{bmatrix}
$$

Substituting $(0, 0, 0)$ for (x, y, z) in the above transform produces $(10, -1, 1)$ for (x', y', z'), which can be confirmed from Figure 7.22. Similarly, substituting $(0, 1, 1)$ for (x, y, z) produces $(10, 0, 0)$ for (x', y', z'), which is also correct.

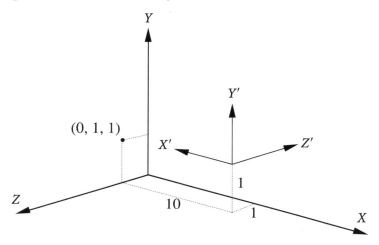

Figure 7.22 *The secondary axial system is subject to a yaw of 180° and an offset of (10, 1, 1).*

Euler angles

Another approach for locating the virtual camera involves Euler angles, but we must remember that they suffer from gimbal lock (see page 95). However, if the virtual camera is located in world space using Euler angles, the transform relating world coordinates to camera coordinates can be derived from the inverse operations. The *yaw, pitch, roll* matrices described above are called *orthogonal matrices*, as the inverse matrix is the transpose of the original rows and columns. Consequently, to rotate through angles $-roll$, $-pitch$ and $-yaw$, we use

- rotate $-roll$ about the z-axis:

$$\begin{bmatrix} \cos(roll) & \sin(roll) & 0 & 0 \\ -\sin(roll) & \cos(roll) & 0 & 0 \\ 0 & 0 & 1 & 0 \\ 0 & 0 & 0 & 1 \end{bmatrix} \tag{7.78}$$

- rotate $-pitch$ about the x-axis:

$$\begin{bmatrix} 1 & 0 & 0 & 0 \\ 0 & \cos(pitch) & \sin(pitch) & 0 \\ 0 & -\sin(pitch) & \cos(pitch) & 0 \\ 0 & 0 & 0 & 1 \end{bmatrix} \tag{7.79}$$

- rotate $-yaw$ about the y-axis:

$$\begin{bmatrix} \cos(yaw) & 0 & -\sin(yaw) & 0 \\ 0 & 1 & 0 & 0 \\ \sin(yaw) & 0 & \cos(yaw) & 0 \\ 0 & 0 & 0 & 1 \end{bmatrix} \tag{7.80}$$

The same result is obtained simply by substituting $-roll$, $-pitch$, $-yaw$ in the original matrices. As described above, the virtual camera will normally be translated from the origin by (t_x, t_y, t_z), which implies that the transform from the world space to the camera space must be evaluated as follows:

$$\begin{bmatrix} x' \\ y' \\ z' \\ 1 \end{bmatrix} = [-roll] \cdot [-pitch] \cdot [-yaw] \cdot [-translate(-t_x, -t_y, -t_z) \cdot \begin{bmatrix} x \\ y \\ z \\ 1 \end{bmatrix} \tag{7.81}$$

which can be represented by a single homogeneous matrix:

$$\begin{bmatrix} x' \\ y' \\ z' \\ 1 \end{bmatrix} = \begin{bmatrix} T_{11} & T_{12} & T_{13} & T_{14} \\ T_{21} & T_{22} & T_{23} & T_{24} \\ T_{31} & T_{32} & T_{33} & T_{34} \\ T_{41} & T_{42} & T_{43} & T_{44} \end{bmatrix} \cdot \begin{bmatrix} x \\ y \\ z \\ 1 \end{bmatrix} \tag{7.82}$$

where

$T_{11} = \cos(yaw)\cos(roll) + \sin(yaw)\sin(pitch)\sin(roll)$

$T_{12} = \cos(pitch)\sin(roll)$

$T_{13} = -\sin(yaw)\cos(roll) + \cos(yaw)\sin(pitch)\sin(roll)$

$T_{14} = -(t_x T_{11} + t_y T_{12} + t_z T_{13})$

$T_{21} = -\cos(yaw)\sin(roll) + \sin(yaw)\sin(pitch)\cos(roll)$

$T_{22} = \cos(pitch)\cos(roll)$

$T_{23} = \sin(yaw)\sin(roll) + \cos(yaw)\sin(pitch)\cos(roll)$

$T_{24} = -(t_x T_{21} + t_y T_{22} + t_z T_{23})$

$T_{31} = \sin(yaw)\cos(pitch)$

$T_{32} = -\sin(pitch)$

$T_{33} = \cos(yaw)\cos(pitch)$

$T_{34} = -(t_x T_{31} + t_y T_{32} + t_z T_{33})$

$T_{41} = 0$

$T_{42} = 0$

$T_{43} = 0$

$T_{44} = 1$ $\tag{7.83}$

This, too, can be verified by a simple example. For instance, consider the situation shown in Figure 7.22 where the following conditions prevail:

$roll$ $= 0°$
$pitch$ $= 0°$
yaw $= 180°$
t_x $= 10$
t_y $= 1$
t_z $= 1$

The transform is

$$\begin{bmatrix} x' \\ y' \\ z' \\ 1 \end{bmatrix} = \begin{bmatrix} -1 & 0 & 0 & 10 \\ 0 & 1 & 0 & -1 \\ 0 & 0 & -1 & 1 \\ 0 & 0 & 0 & 1 \end{bmatrix} \cdot \begin{bmatrix} x \\ y \\ z \\ 1 \end{bmatrix}$$

which is identical to the equation used for direction cosines. Another example is shown in Figure 7.23, where the following conditions exist:

$roll$ = 90°
$pitch$ = 180°
yaw = 0°
t_x = 0.5
t_y = 0.5
t_z = 11

The transform is

$$\begin{bmatrix} x' \\ y' \\ z' \\ 1 \end{bmatrix} = \begin{bmatrix} 0 & -1 & 0 & 0.5 \\ -1 & 0 & 0 & 0.5 \\ 0 & 0 & -1 & 11 \\ 0 & 0 & 0 & 1 \end{bmatrix} \cdot \begin{bmatrix} x \\ y \\ z \\ 1 \end{bmatrix}$$

Substituting $(1, 1, 1)$ for (x, y, z) produces $(-0.5, -0.5, 10)$ for (x', y', z'). Similarly, substituting $(0, 0, 1)$ for (x, y, z) produces $(0.5, 0.5, 10)$ for (x', y', z'), which can be visually verified from Figure 7.23.

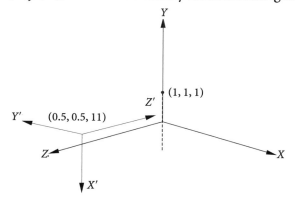

Figure 7.23 *The secondary axial system is subjected to a roll of 90°, a pitch of 180°, and a translation of (0.5, 0.5, 11).*

Quaternions

As mentioned earlier, quaternions were invented by Sir William Rowan Hamilton in the mid 19th century. Sir William was looking for a way to represent complex numbers in higher dimensions, and it took 15 years of toil before he stumbled upon the idea of using a 4D notation – hence the name 'quaternion'.

Since this discovery, mathematicians have shown that quaternions can be used to rotate points about an arbitrary axis, and hence the orientation of objects and the virtual camera. In order to develop the equation that performs this transformation we will have to understand the action of quaternions in the context of rotations.

A quaternion $\mathbf{q}$ is a quadruple of real numbers and is defined as

$$\mathbf{q} = [s, \mathbf{v}] \tag{7.84}$$

where s is a scalar and $\mathbf{v}$ is a 3D vector. If we express the vector $\mathbf{v}$ in terms of its components, we have in an algebraic form

$$\mathbf{q} = [s + x\mathbf{i} + y\mathbf{j} + z\mathbf{k}] \tag{7.85}$$

where s, x, y and z are real numbers.

Adding and subtracting quaternions

Given two quaternions $\mathbf{q}_1$ and $\mathbf{q}_2$,

$$\mathbf{q}_1 = [s_1, \mathbf{v}_1] = [s_1 + x_1\mathbf{i} + y_1\mathbf{j} + z_1\mathbf{k}]$$
$$\mathbf{q}_2 = [s_2, \mathbf{v}_2] = [s_2 + x_2\mathbf{i} + y_2\mathbf{j} + z_2\mathbf{k}] \tag{7.86}$$

they are equal if, and only if, their corresponding terms are equal. Furthermore, like vectors, they can be added and subtracted as follows:

$$\mathbf{q}_1 \pm \mathbf{q}_2 = [(s_1 \pm s_2) + (x_1 \pm x_2)\mathbf{i} + (y_1 \pm y_2)\mathbf{j} + (z_1 \pm z_2)\mathbf{k}] \tag{7.87}$$

Multiplying quaternions

Hamilton discovered that special rules must be used when multiplying quaternions:

$$i^2 = j^2 = k^2 = ijk = -1$$

$$ij = k, jk = i, ki = j$$

$$ji = -k, kj = -i, ik = -j \qquad (7.88)$$

Note that although quaternion addition is commutative, the rules make quaternion multiplication non-commutative.

Given two quaternions q_1 and q_2,

$$q_1 = [s_1, v_1] = [s_1 + x_1 i + y_1 j + z_1 k]$$

$$q_2 = [s_2, v_2] = [s_2 + x_2 i + y_2 j + z_2 k] \qquad (7.89)$$

the product $q_1 q_2$, is given by

$$q_1 q_2 = [(s_1 s_2 - x_1 x_2 - y_1 y_2 - z_1 z_2)$$

$$+ (s_1 x_2 + s_2 x_1 + y_1 z_2 - y_2 z_1)i$$

$$+ (s_1 y_2 + s_2 y_1 + z_1 x_2 - z_2 x_1)j$$

$$+ (s_1 z_2 + s_2 z_1 + x_1 y_2 - x_2 y_1)k \qquad (7.90)$$

which can be rewritten using the dot and cross product notation as

$$q_1 q_2 = [(s_1 s_2 - v_1 \cdot v_2), \; s_1 v_2 + s_2 v_1 + v_1 \times v_2] \qquad (7.91)$$

The inverse quaternion

Given the quaternion

$$q = [s + xi + yj + zk] \qquad (7.92)$$

the inverse quaternion q^{-1} is

$$q^{-1} = \frac{[s - xi - yj - zk]}{|q|^2} \qquad (7.93)$$

where $|\mathbf{q}|$ is the magnitude, or modulus, of $\mathbf{q}$, and is equal to

$$|\mathbf{q}| = \sqrt{s^2 + x^2 + y^2 + z^2} \qquad (7.94)$$

It can also be shown that

$$\mathbf{q}\mathbf{q}^{-1} = \mathbf{q}^{-1}\mathbf{q} = [1 + 0\mathbf{i} + 0\mathbf{j} + 0\mathbf{k}] = 1 \qquad (7.95)$$

Rotating points about an axis

Basically, quaternions are associated with vectors rather than individual points. Therefore, in order to manipulate a single vertex, we must first turn it into a position vector, which has its tail vertex at the origin. A vertex can then be represented in quaternion form by its equivalent position vector and a zero scalar term. For example, a point $P(x, y, z)$ is represented in quaternion form by

$$\mathbf{p} = [0 + x\mathbf{i} + y\mathbf{j} + z\mathbf{k}] \qquad (7.96)$$

which can then be transformed into another position vector using the process described below. The coordinates of the rotated point are the components of the rotated position vector. This may seem an indirect process, but in reality it turns out to be rather simple. Let's now consider how this is achieved.

It can be shown that a position vector $\mathbf{p}$ can be rotated about an axis by some angle using the following operation:

$$\mathbf{p}' = \mathbf{q}\mathbf{p}\mathbf{q}^{-1} \qquad (7.97)$$

where the axis and angle of rotation are encoded within the unit quaternion $\mathbf{q}$, whose modulus is 1, and $\mathbf{p}'$ is the rotated vector. For example, to rotate a point $P(x, y, z)$ through an angle θ about an axis $\mathbf{u}$, we use the following steps:

1 Convert the point $P(x, y, z)$ to a quaternion $\mathbf{p}$:

$$\mathbf{p} = [0 + x\mathbf{i} + y\mathbf{j} + z\mathbf{k}]$$

2 Define the axis of rotation as a unit vector $\mathbf{u}$:

$$\mathbf{u} = [x_u\mathbf{i} + y_u\mathbf{j} + z_u\mathbf{k}]$$

3 Define the transforming quaternion **q**:

$$\mathbf{q} = [\cos(\theta/2), \sin(\theta/2)\mathbf{u}]$$

4 Define the inverse of the transforming quaternion $\mathbf{q}^{-1}$:

$$\mathbf{q}^{-1} = [\cos(\theta/2), -\sin(\theta/2)\mathbf{u}]$$

5 Compute **p**′:

$$\mathbf{p}' = \mathbf{q}\mathbf{p}\mathbf{q}^{-1}$$

6 Unpack (x', y', z')

$$(x', y', z') \quad \mathbf{p}' = [0 + x'\mathbf{i} + y'\mathbf{j} + z'\mathbf{k}]$$

We can verify the action of the above transform with a simple example. Consider the point $P(0, 1, 1)$ in Figure 7.24 which is to be rotated 90° about the y-axis. We can see that the rotated point P' has the coordinates $(1, 1, 0)$, which we will confirm algebraically. The point P is represented by a quaternion **P**, and is rotated by evaluating the quaternion **P**′:

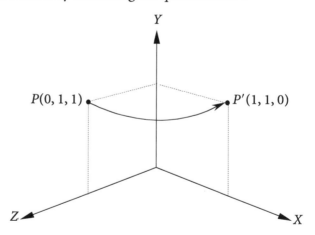

Figure 7.24 The point $P(0, 1, 1)$ is rotated to $P'(1, 1, 0)$ using a quaternion coincident with the y-axis.

$$\mathbf{P}' = \mathbf{q}\mathbf{P}\mathbf{q}^{-1}$$

which will store the rotated coordinates. The axis of rotation is $[0\mathbf{i} + 1\mathbf{j} + 0\mathbf{k}]$, therefore the unit quaternion **q** is given by

$$\mathbf{q} = [\cos(90°/2), \sin(90°/2)[0, 1, 0]]$$

$$= [\cos(45°), [0, \sin(45°), 0]]$$

The inverse quaternion $\mathbf{q}^{-1}$ is given by

$$\mathbf{q}^{-1} = \frac{[\cos(90°/2), -\sin(90°/2)[0, 1, 0]]}{|\mathbf{q}|^2}$$

but as $\mathbf{q}$ is a unit quaternion, the denominator $|\mathbf{q}|^2$ equals unity and can be ignored. Therefore

$$\mathbf{q}^{-1} = [\cos(45°), [0, -\sin(45°)\ 0]]$$

Let's evaluate $\mathbf{qPq}^{-1}$ in two stages: $(\mathbf{qP})\mathbf{q}^{-1}$.

1

$$\mathbf{qP} = [\cos(45°), [0, \sin(45°), 0]] \cdot [0, [0, 1, 1]]$$

$$= [-\sin(45°), [\sin(45°), \cos(45°), \cos(45°)]]$$

2

$$(\mathbf{qP})\mathbf{q}^{-1} = [-\sin(45°), [\sin(45°), \cos(45°), \cos(45°)]] \cdot$$

$$[\cos(45°), [0, -\sin(45°), 0]]$$

$$= [0, [2\sin(45°)\cos(45°), 1, \cos(45°)\cos(45°) - \sin(45°)\sin(45°)]]$$

$$P' = [0, [1, 1, 0]]$$

and the vector component of P' confirms that P is indeed rotated to $(1, 1, 0)$.

We will evaluate one more example before continuing. Consider a rotation about the z-axis as illustrated in Figure 7.25. The original point has coordinates $(0, 1, 1)$ and is rotated $-90°$. From the figure we see that this should finish at $(1, 0, 1)$.

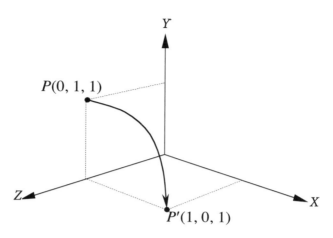

Figure 7.25 *The point P(0, 1, 1) is rotated −90° to P' (1, 0, 1) using a quaternion coincident with the z-axis*

This time the quaternion **q** is defined by

$$\mathbf{q} = [\cos(-90°/2), \sin(-90°/2)[0, 0, 1]]$$

$$= [\cos(45°), [0, 0, -\sin(45°)]]$$

with its inverse

$$\mathbf{q}^{-1} = [\cos(45°), [0, 0, \sin(45°)]]$$

and the point to be rotated in quaternion form is $\mathbf{P} = [0, [0, 1, 1]]$. Evaluating this in two stages we have

1

$$\mathbf{qP} = [\cos(45°), [0, 0, -\sin(45°)]] \cdot [0, [0, 1, 1]]$$

$$= [\sin(45°), [\sin(45°), \cos(45°), \cos(45°)]]$$

2

$$(\mathbf{pP})\mathbf{q}^{-1} = [\sin(45°), [\sin(45°), \cos(45°), \cos(45°)]] \cdot [\cos(45°), [0, 0, \sin(45°)]]$$

$$= [0, [\sin(90°), \cos(90°), 1]]$$

The vector component of P' confirms that P is rotated to $(1, 0, 1)$.

Roll, pitch and yaw quaternions

Having already looked at roll, pitch and yaw rotations, we can now define them as quaternions:

$$\mathbf{q}_{roll} = [\cos(\theta/2), \sin(\theta/2)[0, 0, 1]]$$

$$\mathbf{q}_{pitch} = [\cos(\theta/2), \sin(\theta/2)[1, 0, 0]]$$

$$\mathbf{q}_{yaw} = [\cos(\theta/2), \sin(\theta/2)[0, 1, 0]] \qquad (7.98)$$

where θ is the angle of rotation.

These quaternions can be multiplied together to create a single quaternion representing a compound rotation. For example, if the quaternions are defined as

$$\mathbf{q}_{roll} = [\cos(roll/2), \sin(roll/2)[0, 0, 1]]$$

$$\mathbf{q}_{pitch} = [\cos(pitch/2), \sin(pitch/2)[1, 0, 0]]$$

$$\mathbf{q}_{yaw} = [\cos(yaw/2), \sin(yaw/2)[0, 1, 0]] \qquad (7.99)$$

they can be concatenated to a single quaternion $\mathbf{q}$:

$$\mathbf{q} = \mathbf{q}_{yaw}\mathbf{q}_{pitch}\mathbf{q}_{roll} = [s + x\mathbf{i} + y\mathbf{j} + z\mathbf{k}] \qquad (7.100)$$

where

$$s = \cos(\tfrac{yaw}{2})\cos(\tfrac{pitch}{2})\cos(\tfrac{roll}{2}) + \sin(\tfrac{yaw}{2})\sin(\tfrac{pitch}{2})\sin(\tfrac{roll}{2})$$

$$x = \cos(\tfrac{yaw}{2})\sin(\tfrac{pitch}{2})\cos(\tfrac{roll}{2}) + \sin(\tfrac{yaw}{2})\cos(\tfrac{pitch}{2})\sin(\tfrac{roll}{2})$$

$$y = \sin(\tfrac{yaw}{2})\cos(\tfrac{pitch}{2})\cos(\tfrac{roll}{2}) - \cos(\tfrac{yaw}{2})\sin(\tfrac{pitch}{2})\sin(\tfrac{roll}{2})$$

$$z = \cos(\tfrac{yaw}{2})\cos(\tfrac{pitch}{2})\sin(\tfrac{roll}{2}) - \sin(\tfrac{yaw}{2})\sin(\tfrac{pitch}{2})\cos(\tfrac{roll}{2})$$

$$(7.101)$$

Let's examine this compound quaternion with an example. For instance, given the following conditions let's derive a single quaternion $\mathbf{q}$ to represent the compound rotation:

$roll = 90°$
$pitch = 180°$
$yaw = 0°$

The values of s, x, y, z are

$s = 0$
$x = \cos(45°)$
$y = -\sin(45°)$
$z = 0$

and the quaternion **q** is

$\mathbf{q} = [0, [\cos(45°), -\sin(45°), 0]]$

If the point $P(1, 1, 1)$ is subjected to this compound rotation, the rotated point is computed using the standard quaternion transform:

$\mathbf{P'} = \mathbf{q}\mathbf{P}\mathbf{q}^{-1}$

Let's evaluate $\mathbf{q}\mathbf{P}\mathbf{q}^{-1}$ in two stages:

1

$\mathbf{q}\mathbf{P} = [0, [\cos(45°), -\sin(45°), 0]] \cdot [0, [1, 1, 1]]$

$\quad = [0, [-\sin(45°), -\cos(45°), \sin(45°) + \cos(45°)]]$

2

$(\mathbf{q}\mathbf{P})\mathbf{q}^{-1} = [0, [-\sin(45°), -\cos(45°), \sin(45°) + \cos(45°)]] \cdot$
$[0, [-\cos(45°), \sin(45°), 0]]$

$\mathbf{P'} = [0, [-1, -1, -1]]$

Therefore, the coordinates of the rotated point are $(-1, -1, -1)$, which can be confirmed from Figure 7.26.

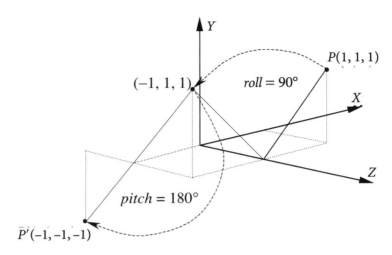

Figure 7.26 *The point P is subject to a compound roll of 90° and a pitch of 180°. This diagram shows the transform in two stages.*

Quaternions in matrix form

There is a direct relationship between quaternions and matrices. For example, given the quaternion $[s + x\mathbf{i} + y\mathbf{j} + z\mathbf{k})$ the equivalent matrix is

$$\begin{bmatrix} M_{11} & M_{12} & M_{13} \\ M_{21} & M_{22} & M_{23} \\ M_{31} & M_{32} & M_{33} \end{bmatrix}$$

where

$M_{11} = 1 - 2(y^2 + z^2)$

$M_{12} = 2(xy - sz)$

$M_{13} = 2(xz + sy)$

$M_{21} = 2(xy + sz)$

$M_{22} = 1 - 2(x^2 + z^2)$

$M_{23} = 2(yz + sx)$

$M_{31} = 2(xz + sy)$

$M_{32} = 2(yz + sx)$

$M_{33} = 1 - 2(x^2 + y^2)$ (7.102)

Substituting the following values of s, x, y, z:

$s = 0$

$x = \cos(45°)$

$y = -\sin(45°)$

$z = 0$

the matrix transformation is

$$\begin{bmatrix} x' \\ y' \\ z' \end{bmatrix} = \begin{bmatrix} 0 & -1 & 0 \\ -1 & 0 & 0 \\ 0 & 0 & -1 \end{bmatrix} \cdot \begin{bmatrix} x \\ y \\ z \end{bmatrix}$$

Substituting $(1, 1, 1)$ for (x, y, z) the rotated point becomes $(-1, -1, -1)$, as shown in Figure 7.26.

Frames of reference

A quaternion, or its equivalent matrix, can be used to rotate a vertex or position a virtual camera. If unit quaternions are used, the associated matrix is orthogonal, which means that its transpose is equivalent to rotating the frame of reference in the opposite direction. For example, if the virtual camera is oriented with a yaw rotation of 180°, i.e. looking along the negative z-axis, the orientation quaternion is $[0, [0, 1, 0]]$. Therefore $s = 0$, $x = 0$, $y = 1$, $z = 0$. The equivalent matrix is

$$\begin{bmatrix} -1 & 0 & 0 \\ 0 & 1 & 0 \\ 0 & 0 & -1 \end{bmatrix}$$

which is equal to its transpose. Therefore, a vertex (x, y, z) in world space has coordinates (x', y', z') in camera space and the transform is defined by

$$\begin{bmatrix} x' \\ y' \\ z' \end{bmatrix} = \begin{bmatrix} -1 & 0 & 0 \\ 0 & 1 & 0 \\ 0 & 0 & -1 \end{bmatrix} \cdot \begin{bmatrix} x \\ y \\ z \end{bmatrix}$$

If the vertex (x, y, z) is $(1, 1, 0)$, (x', y', z') becomes $(-1, 1, 0)$, which is correct. However, it is unlikely that the virtual camera will only be subjected to a simple rotation, as it will normally be translated from the origin. Consequently, a translation matrix will have to be introduced as described above.

Transforming vectors

The transforms described in this chapter have been used to transform single points. However, a geometric database will contain not only pure vertices, but also vectors, which must also be subject to any prevailing transform. A generic transform Q of a 3D point can be represented by

$$\begin{bmatrix} x' \\ y' \\ z' \\ 1 \end{bmatrix} = [Q] \cdot \begin{bmatrix} x \\ y \\ z \\ 1 \end{bmatrix} \tag{7.103}$$

and as a vector is defined by two points we can write

$$\begin{bmatrix} x' \\ y' \\ z' \\ 1 \end{bmatrix} = [Q] \cdot \begin{bmatrix} x_2 - x_1 \\ y_2 - y_1 \\ z_2 - z_1 \\ 1 - 1 \end{bmatrix} \tag{7.104}$$

where we see the homogeneous scaling term collapse to zero. This implies that any vector $[x\,y\,z]^{\mathrm{T}}$ can be transformed using

$$\begin{bmatrix} x' \\ y' \\ z' \\ 0 \end{bmatrix} = [Q] \cdot \begin{bmatrix} x \\ y \\ z \\ 0 \end{bmatrix} \tag{7.105}$$

Let's put this to the test by using a transform from an earlier example. The problem concerned a change of axial system where a virtual camera was subject to the following:

$roll$ = 180°
$pitch$ = 90°
yaw = 90°
t_x = 2
t_y = 2
t_z = 0

and the transform is

$$\begin{bmatrix} x' \\ y' \\ z' \\ 1 \end{bmatrix} = \begin{bmatrix} 0 & -1 & 0 & 2 \\ 0 & 0 & 1 & 0 \\ -1 & 0 & 0 & 2 \\ 0 & 0 & 0 & 1 \end{bmatrix} \cdot \begin{bmatrix} x \\ y \\ z \\ 1 \end{bmatrix}$$

When the point $(1, 1, 0)$ is transformed it becomes $(1, 0, 1)$, as shown in Figure 7.27. But if we transform the vector $[1\ 1\ 0]^T$ it becomes $[-1\ 0\ -1]^T$, using the following transform

$$\begin{bmatrix} -1 \\ 0 \\ -1 \\ 0 \end{bmatrix} = \begin{bmatrix} 0 & -1 & 0 & 2 \\ 0 & 0 & 1 & 0 \\ -1 & 0 & 0 & 2 \\ 0 & 0 & 0 & 1 \end{bmatrix} \cdot \begin{bmatrix} 1 \\ 1 \\ 0 \\ 0 \end{bmatrix}$$

which is correct with reference to Figure 7.27.

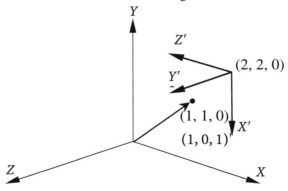

Figure 7.27 *Vector $[1\ 1\ 0]^T$ is transformed to $[-1\ 0\ -1]^T$.*

Determinants

Before concluding this chapter I would like to expand upon the role of the determinant in transforms. Normally, determinants arise in the solution of linear equations such as

$$c_1 = a_1 x + b_1 y$$

$$c_2 = a_2 x + b_2 y \qquad (7.106)$$

where values of x and y are defined in terms of the other constants. Without showing the solution, the values of x and y are given by

$$x = \frac{c_1 b_2 - c_2 b_1}{a_1 b_2 - a_2 b_1}$$

$$y = \frac{a_1 c_2 - a_2 c_1}{a_1 b_2 - a_2 b_1} \qquad (7.107)$$

provided that the denominator $a_1 b_2 - a_2 b_1 \neq 0$.

It is also possible to write the linear equations in matrix form as

$$\begin{bmatrix} c_1 \\ c_2 \end{bmatrix} = \begin{bmatrix} a_1 & b_1 \\ a_2 & b_2 \end{bmatrix} \cdot \begin{bmatrix} x \\ y \end{bmatrix} \qquad (7.108)$$

and we notice that the denominator comes from the matrix terms $a_1 b_2 - a_2 b_1$. This is called the *determinant,* and is valid only for square matrices. A determinant is defined as follows:

$$\begin{vmatrix} a_1 & b_1 \\ a_2 & b_2 \end{vmatrix} = a_1 b_2 - a_2 b_1 \qquad (7.109)$$

With this notation it is possible to rewrite the original linear equations as

$$\frac{x}{\begin{vmatrix} c_1 & b_1 \\ c_2 & b_2 \end{vmatrix}} = \frac{y}{\begin{vmatrix} a_1 & c_1 \\ a_2 & c_2 \end{vmatrix}} = \frac{1}{\begin{vmatrix} a_1 & b_1 \\ a_2 & b_2 \end{vmatrix}} \qquad (7.110)$$

With a set of three linear equations:

$$d_1 = a_1x + b_1y + c_1z$$

$$d_2 = a_2x + b_2y + c_2z$$

$$d_3 = a_3x + b_3y + c_3z \qquad (7.111)$$

the value of x is defined as

$$x = \frac{d_1b_2c_3 - d_1b_3c_2 + d_2b_3c_1 - d_2b_1c_3 + d_3b_1c_2 - d_3b_2c_1}{a_1b_2c_3 - a_1b_3c_2 + a_2b_3c_1 - a_2b_1c_3 + a_3b_1c_2 - a_3b_2c_1} \qquad (7.112)$$

with similar expressions for y and z. Once more, the denominator comes from the determinant of the matrix associated with the matrix formulation of the linear equations:

$$\begin{bmatrix} d_1 \\ d_2 \\ d_3 \end{bmatrix} = \begin{bmatrix} a_1 & b_1 & c_1 \\ a_2 & b_2 & c_2 \\ a_3 & b_3 & c_3 \end{bmatrix} \cdot \begin{bmatrix} x \\ y \\ z \end{bmatrix} \qquad (7.113)$$

where

$$\begin{vmatrix} a_1 & b_1 & c_1 \\ a_2 & b_2 & c_2 \\ a_3 & b_3 & c_3 \end{vmatrix} = a_1b_2c_3 - a_1b_3c_2 + a_2b_3c_1 - a_2b_1c_3 + a_3b_1c_2 - a_3b_2c_1$$

which can be written as

$$a_1 \begin{vmatrix} b_2 & c_2 \\ b_3 & c_3 \end{vmatrix} - a_2 \begin{vmatrix} b_1 & c_1 \\ b_3 & c_3 \end{vmatrix} + a_3 \begin{vmatrix} b_1 & c_1 \\ b_2 & c_2 \end{vmatrix} \qquad (7.114)$$

Let's now see what creates a zero determinant. If we write, for example

$$10 = 2x + y \qquad (7.115)$$

there are an infinite number of solutions for x and y, and it is impossible to solve the equation. However, if we introduce a second equation relating x and y:

$$4 = 5x - y \qquad (7.116)$$

we can solve for x and y using (7.107):

$$x = \frac{10 \times (-1) - 4 \times 1}{2 \times (-1) - 5 \times 1} = \frac{-14}{-7} = 2$$

$$y = \frac{2 \times 4 - 5 \times 10}{2 \times (-1) - 5 \times 1} = \frac{-42}{-7} = 6 \qquad (7.117)$$

therefore $x = 2$ and $y = 6$, which is correct.

But say the second equation had been

$$20 = 4x + 2y \qquad (7.118)$$

which would have created the pair of simultaneous equations

$$10 = 2x + y \qquad (7.119)$$

$$20 = 4x + 2y \qquad (7.120)$$

If we now solve for x and y we get

$$x = \frac{10 \times 2 - 20 \times 1}{2 \times 2 - 4 \times 1} = \frac{0}{0} = \text{undefined}$$

$$y = \frac{2 \times 20 - 4 \times 10}{2 \times 2 - 4 \times 1} = \frac{0}{0} = \text{undefined}$$

which yields undefined results. The reason for this is that (7.119) is the same as (7.120) – the second equation is nothing more than twice the first equation, and therefore brings nothing new to the relationship. When this occurs, the equations are said to be *linearly dependent*.

Having shown the algebraic origins of the determinant, we can now go on to investigate its graphical significance. Consider the transform

$$\begin{bmatrix} x' \\ y' \end{bmatrix} = \begin{bmatrix} a & b \\ c & d \end{bmatrix} \cdot \begin{bmatrix} x \\ y \end{bmatrix} \qquad (7.121)$$

The determinant of the transform is $ad - cb$. If we subject the vertices of a unit-square to this transform, we create the situation shown in Figure 7.28. The vertices of the unit-square are moved as follows:

$$\begin{array}{ll}
(0,0) & (0,0) \\
(1,0) & (a,c) \\
(1,1) & (a+b,c+d) \\
(0,1) & (b,d)
\end{array} \tag{7.122}$$

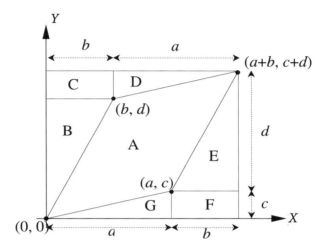

Figure 7.28 *The inner parallelogram is the transformed unit square.*

From Figure 7.28 it can be seen that the area of the transformed unit-square A' is given by

$$area = (a+b)(c+d) - B - C - D - E - F - G$$

$$= ac + ad + cb + bd - \tfrac{1}{2}bd - cb - \tfrac{1}{2}ac - \tfrac{1}{2}bd - cb - \tfrac{1}{2}ac$$

$$= ad - cb \tag{7.123}$$

which is the determinant of the transform. But as the area of the original unit-square was 1, the determinant of the transform controls the scaling factor applied to the transformed shape.

Let's examine the determinants of two transforms. The first 2D transform encodes a scaling of 2, and results in an overall area scaling of 4:

$$\begin{bmatrix} 2 & 0 \\ 0 & 2 \end{bmatrix} \text{ and the determinant is } \begin{vmatrix} 2 & 0 \\ 0 & 2 \end{vmatrix} = 4$$

The second 2D transform encodes a scaling of 3 and a translation of $(3, 3)$, and results in an overall area scaling of 9:

$$\begin{bmatrix} 3 & 0 & 3 \\ 0 & 3 & 3 \\ 0 & 0 & 1 \end{bmatrix}$$ and the determinant is

$$3\begin{vmatrix} 3 & 3 \\ 0 & 1 \end{vmatrix} - 0\begin{vmatrix} 0 & 3 \\ 0 & 1 \end{vmatrix} + 0\begin{vmatrix} 0 & 3 \\ 3 & 3 \end{vmatrix} = 9$$

These two examples demonstrate the extra role played by the elements of a matrix.

Perspective projection

Of all the projections employed in computer graphics, the *perspective projection* is the one most widely used. There are two stages to its computation: the first stage involves converting world coordinates to the camera's frame of reference, and the second stage transforms camera coordinates to the projection plane coordinates. We have already looked at the transforms for locating a camera in world space, and the inverse transform for converting world coordinates to the camera's frame of reference. Let's now investigate how these camera coordinates are transformed into a perspective projection.

We begin by assuming that the camera is directed along the z-axis as shown in Figure 7.29. Positioned d units along the axis is a projection screen, which will be used to capture a perspective projection of an object. Figure 7.29 shows that any point (x_c, y_c, z_c) becomes transformed to (x_s, y_s, d). It also shows that the screen's x-axis is pointing in the opposite direction to the camera's x-axis, which can be compensated for by reversing the sign of x_s when it is computed.

Figure 7.30 shows plan and side views of the scenario depicted in Figure 7.29, which enables us to inspect the geometry and make the following observations:

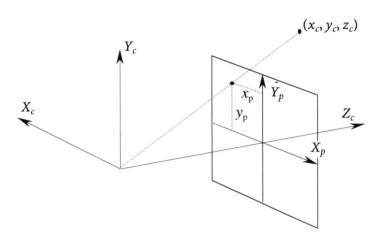

Figure 7.29 *The axial systems used to produce a perspective projection.*

$$\frac{x}{z} = \frac{-x_p}{d} \quad x_p = -d\frac{x}{z} \quad x_p = \frac{-y}{z/d}$$

$$\frac{y}{z} = \frac{y_p}{d} \quad y_p = d\frac{y}{z} \quad y_p = \frac{y}{z/d} \tag{7.124}$$

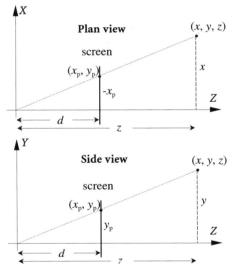

Figure 7.30 *The plan and side views for computing the perspective projection transform.*

This can be expressed in matrix form as

$$
\begin{bmatrix} x_s \\ y_s \\ z_s \\ W \end{bmatrix} = \begin{bmatrix} -1 & 0 & 0 & 0 \\ 0 & 1 & 0 & 0 \\ 0 & 0 & 1 & 0 \\ 0 & 0 & 1/d & 0 \end{bmatrix} \cdot \begin{bmatrix} x \\ y \\ z \\ 1 \end{bmatrix}
$$

At first this may seem strange, but if we multiply it out we get

$$[x_p \ y_p \ z_p \ W]^T = [-x \ y \ z \ z/d]^T$$

and if we remember the idea behind homogeneous coordinates, we must divide the terms x_p, y_p, z_p by W to get the scaled terms, which produces

$$x_p = \frac{-x}{z/d}, \quad y_p = \frac{y}{z/d}, \quad z_p = \frac{z}{z/d} = d$$

which, after all, is rather elegant. Notice that this transform takes into account the sign change that occurs with the x-coordinate. Some books will leave this sign reversal until the mapping is made to screen coordinates.

Summary

The purpose of this chapter was to introduce transforms and matrices – I hope this has been achieved. This end of the chapter is not really the end of the subject, as one can do so much with matrices and quaternions. For example, it would be interesting to see how a matrix behaves when some of its elements are changed dynamically, and what happens when we interpolate between a pair of quaternions. Such topics are addressed in later chapters.

Chapter

8

Interpolation

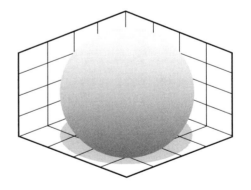

Interpolation is not a branch of mathematics but rather a collection of techniques the reader will find useful when solving computer graphics problems. Basically, an *interpolant* is a way of changing one number into another. For example, to change 2 into 4 we simply add 2, which is not very useful. The real function of an interpolant is to change one number into another in, perhaps, 10 equal steps. Thus if we start with 2 and repeatedly add 0.2, this generates the sequence 2.2, 2.4, 2.6, 2.8, 3.0, 3.2, 3.4, 3.6, 3.8 and 4. These numbers could then be used to translate, scale, rotate an object, move a virtual camera, or change the position, colour or brightness of a virtual light source.

In order to repeat the above interpolant for different numbers we require a formula, which is one of the first exercises of this chapter. We also need to explore ways of controlling the spacing between the interpolated values. In animation, for example, we often need to move an object very slowly and gradually increase its speed. Conversely, we may want to bring an object to a halt, making its speed less and less.

We start with the simplest of all interpolants: the linear interpolant.

Linear interpolant

A *linear interpolant* generates equal spacing between the interpolated values for equal changes in the interpolating parameter. In the introductory example the increment 0.2 is calculated by subtracting the first number from the second and dividing the result by 10, i.e. $(4-2)/10 = 0.2$. Although this works, it is not in a very flexible form, so let's express the problem differently. Given two numbers n_1 and n_2, which represent the start and final values of the interpolant, we require an interpolated value controlled by a parameter t that varies between 0 and 1. When $t = 0$, the result is n_1, and when $t = 1$, the result is n_2. A solution to this problem is given by

$$n = n_1 + t(n_2 - n_1) \tag{8.1}$$

for when $n_1 = 2$, $n_2 = 4$ and $t = 0.5$

$$n = 2 + \tfrac{1}{2}(4 - 2) = 3$$

which is a halfway point. Furthermore, when $t = 0$, $n = n_1$, and when $t = 1$, $n = n_2$, which confirms that we have a sound interpolant. However, it can be expressed differently:

$$n = n_1 + t(n_2 - n_1) \tag{8.2}$$

$$n = n_1 + tn_2 - tn_1 \tag{8.3}$$

$$n = n_1(1 - t) + n_2 t \tag{8.4}$$

which shows what is really going on, and forms the basis for further development. Figure 8.1 shows the graphs of $(1 - t)$ and t over the range 0 to 1.

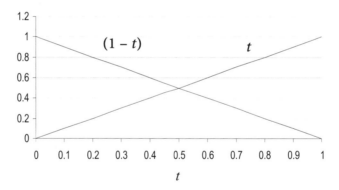

Figure 8.1 *The graphs of $(1-t)$ and t over the range 0 to 1.*

With reference to (8.4), we see that as t changes from 0 to 1, the $(1 - t)$ term varies from 1 to 0. This effectively attenuates the value of n_1 to zero over the range of t, while the t term scales n_2 from zero to its actual value. Figure 8.2 illustrates these two actions with $n_1 = 1$ and $n_2 = 3$. Notice that the terms $(1 - t)$ and t sum to unity; this is not a coincidence. This type of interpolant ensures that if it takes a quarter of n_1, it balances it with three-quarters of n_2, and vice versa. Obviously we could design an interpolant that takes arbitrary portions of n_1 and n_2, but that would lead to arbitrary results.

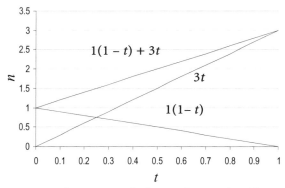

Figure 8.2 *The top graph shows the result of linearly interpolating between values 1 and 3.*

Although this interpolant is extremely simple, it is widely used in computer graphics software. Just to put it into context, consider the task of moving an object between two locations (x_1, y_1, z_1) and (x_2, y_2, z_2). The interpolated position is given by

$$x = x_1(1 - t) + x_2 t$$
$$y = y_1(1 - t) + y_2 t$$
$$z = z_1(1 - t) + z_2 t \qquad (8.5)$$

for $0 \leq t \leq 1$

The parameter t could be generated from two frame values within an animation. What is assured by this interpolant, is that equal steps in t result in equal steps in x, y and z. Figure 8.3 illustrates this linear spacing with a 2D example.

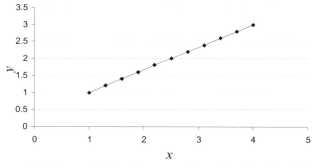

Figure 8.3 *Interpolating between the points (1,1) and (4,3). Note that linear changes in t give rise to equal spaces along the line.*

We can write (8.2) in matrix form as follows:

$$n = \begin{bmatrix} (1-t) & t \end{bmatrix} \cdot \begin{bmatrix} n_1 \\ n_2 \end{bmatrix} \tag{8.6}$$

or

$$n = \begin{bmatrix} t & 1 \end{bmatrix} \cdot \begin{bmatrix} -1 & 1 \\ 1 & 0 \end{bmatrix} \cdot \begin{bmatrix} n_1 \\ n_2 \end{bmatrix} \tag{8.7}$$

The reader can confirm that this generates identical results to the algebraic form.

Non-linear interpolation

A linear interpolant ensures that equal steps in the parameter t give rise to equal steps in the interpolated values; however, it is often required that equal steps in t give rise to unequal steps in the interpolated values. We can achieve this using a variety of mathematical techniques. For example, we could use trigonometric functions or polynomials. To begin with, let's look at a trigonometric solution.

Trigonometric interpolation

In Chapter 4 we noted that $\sin^2(\beta) + \cos^2(\beta) = 1$, which satisfies one of the requirements of an interpolant: the terms must sum to 1. If β varies between 0 and $\pi/2$, $\cos^2(\beta)$ varies between 1 and 0, and $\sin^2(\beta)$ varies between 0 and 1, which can be used to modify the two interpolated values n_1 and n_2 as follows:

$$n = n_1 \cos^2(t) + n_2 \sin^2(t) \tag{8.8}$$

for $0 \leq t \leq \pi/2$

The interpolation curves are shown in Figure 8.4.

If we make $n_1 = 1$ and $n_2 = 3$ in (8.8), we obtain the curves shown in Figure 8.5. If we apply this interpolant to two 2D points in space, (1, 1) and (4, 3), we obtain a straight-line

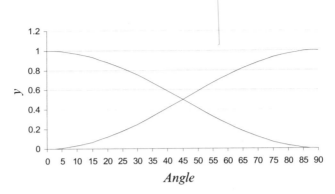

Figure 8.4 *The curves for $\cos^2(\beta)$ and $\sin^2(\beta)$.*

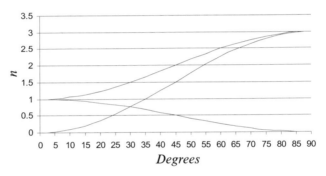

Figure 8.5 *Interpolating between 1 and 3 using a trigonometric interpolant.*

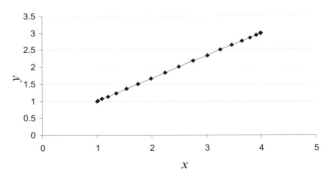

Figure 8.6 *Interpolating between two points (1,1) and (4,3). Note the non-linear distribution of points.*

interpolation, but the distribution of points is non-linear, as shown in Figure 8.6. In other words, equal steps in t give rise to unequal distances.

The main problem with this approach is that it is impossible to change the nature of the curve – it is a *sinusoid*, and its slope is determined by the interpolated values. One way of gaining control over the interpolated curve is to use a *polynomial*, which is the subject of the next section.

Cubic interpolation

To begin with, let's develop a cubic blending function that will be similar to the previous sinusoidal one. This can then be extended to provide extra flexibility. A *cubic polynomial* will form the basis of the interpolant

$$V_1 = at^3 + bt^2 + ct + d \qquad (8.9)$$

and the final interpolant will be of the form

$$n = \begin{bmatrix} V_1 & V_2 \end{bmatrix} \cdot \begin{bmatrix} n_1 \\ n_2 \end{bmatrix} \qquad (8.10)$$

The task is to find the values of the constants associated with the polynomials V_1 and V_2. The requirements are:

1 A cubic function V_2 must grow from 0 to 1 for $0 \le t \le 1$.
2 The slope at a point t, must equal the slope at the point $(1 - t)$. This ensures slope symmetry over the range of the function.
3 The value V_2 at any point t must also produce $(1 - V_2)$ at $(1 - t)$. This ensures curve symmetry.

- To satisfy the first requirement:

$$V_2 = at^3 + bt^2 + ct + d \qquad (8.11)$$

  therefore, $t = 0$, $d = 0$ for $V_2 = 0$, and when $t = 1$, $V_2 = a + b + c$.
- To satisfy the second requirement, we differentiate V_2 to obtain the slope

$$\frac{dV_2}{dt} = 3at^2 + 2bt + c = 3a(1 - t)^2 + 2b(1 - t) + c \qquad (8.12)$$

and equating constants we discover $c = 0$ and $0 = 3a + 2b$

- To satisfy the third requirement,

$$at^3 + bt^2 = 1 - [a(1 - t)^3 + b(1 - t)^2] \qquad (8.13)$$

where we discover $1 = a + b$. But $0 = 3a + 2b$, therefore $a = -2$ and $b = 3$. Therefore

$$V_2 = -2t^3 + 3t^2 \qquad (8.14)$$

To find the curve's mirror curve, which starts at 1 and collapses to 0 as t moves from 0 to 1, we subtract (8.14) from 1:

$$V_1 = 2t^3 - 3t^2 + 1 \qquad (8.15)$$

Therefore, the two polynomials are

$$V_2 = -2t^3 + 3t^2$$
$$V_1 = 2t^3 - 3t^2 + 1 \qquad (8.16)$$

and are shown in Figure 8.7. They can be used as interpolants as follows:

$$n = n_1 V_1 + n_2 V_2 \qquad (8.17)$$

which in matrix form is

$$n = \begin{bmatrix} 2t^3 - 3t^2 + 1 & -2t^3 + 3t^2 \end{bmatrix} \cdot \begin{bmatrix} n_1 \\ n_2 \end{bmatrix} \qquad (8.18)$$

$$n = \begin{bmatrix} t^3 & t^2 & t^1 & 1 \end{bmatrix} \begin{bmatrix} 2 & -2 \\ -3 & 3 \\ 0 & 0 \\ 1 & 0 \end{bmatrix} \cdot \begin{bmatrix} n_1 \\ n_2 \end{bmatrix} \qquad (8.19)$$

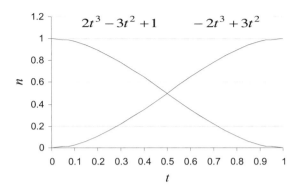

Figure 8.7 *Two cubic interpolants.*

If we let $n_1 = 1$ and $n_2 = 3$ we obtain the curves shown in Figure 8.8. And if we apply the interpolant to the points $(1, 1)$ and $(4, 3)$ we obtain the curves shown in Figure 8.9.

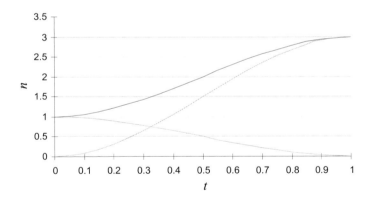

Figure 8.8 *Interpolating between 1 and 3 using a cubic interpolant.*

This interpolant can be used to blend any pair of numbers together. But say we wished to associate other qualities with the numbers n_1 and n_2, such as their tangent vectors s_1 and s_2. Perhaps we could interpolate these alongside n_1 and n_2. In fact this can be done, as we shall see.

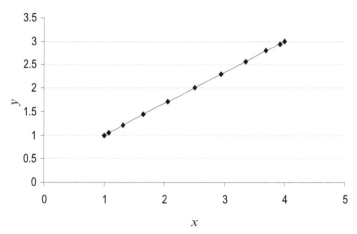

Figure 8.9 *A cubic interpolant between points*
(1, 1) and (4, 3).

The requirement is to modulate the interpolating curve in Figure 8.8 with two further cubic curves. One curve blends out the tangent vector s_1 associated with n_1, and the other blends in the tangent vector s_2 associated with n_2. Let's begin with a cubic polynomial to blend s_1 to zero:

$$V_{out} = at^3 + bt^2 + ct + d \qquad (8.20)$$

V_{out} must equal zero when $t = 0$ and $t = 1$, otherwise it will disturb the start and end values. Therefore $d = 0$, and

$$a + b + c = 0 \qquad (8.21)$$

The rate of change of V_{out} relative to t (i.e. $\dfrac{dV_{out}}{dt}$) must equal 1 when $t = 0$, so it can be used to multiply s_1. When $t = 1$, $\dfrac{dV_{out}}{dt}$ must equal 0 to attenuate any trace of s_1:

$$\frac{dV_{out}}{dt} = 3at^2 + 2bt + c \qquad (8.22)$$

but $\dfrac{dV_{out}}{dt} = 1$ when $t = 0$, and $\dfrac{dV_{out}}{dt} = 0$ when $t = 1$. Therefore $c = 1$, and

$$3a + 2b + 1 = 0 \tag{8.23}$$

But using (8.21) means that $b = -2$ and $a = 1$. Therefore, the polynomial V_{out} has the form

$$V_{\text{out}} = t^3 - 2t^2 + t \tag{8.24}$$

Using a similar argument, one can prove that the function to blend in s_2 equals

$$V_{\text{in}} = t^3 - t^2 \tag{8.25}$$

Graphs of (8.24) and (8.25) are shown alongside graphs of (8.16) in Figure 8.10.

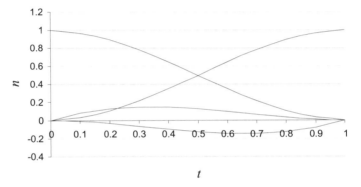

Figure 8.10 *The four Hermite interpolating curves.*

The complete interpolating function looks like

$$n = [2t^3 - 3t^2 + 1 \quad -2t^3 + 3t^2 \quad t^3 - 2t^2 + t \quad t^3 - t^2] \cdot \begin{bmatrix} n_1 \\ n_2 \\ s_1 \\ s_2 \end{bmatrix} \tag{8.26}$$

and, unpacking the constants and polynomial terms, we obtain

$$n = [t^3 \; t^2 \; t^1 \; 1] \cdot \begin{bmatrix} 2 & -2 & 1 & 1 \\ -3 & 3 & -2 & -1 \\ 0 & 0 & 1 & 0 \\ 1 & 0 & 0 & 0 \end{bmatrix} \cdot \begin{bmatrix} n_1 \\ n_2 \\ s_1 \\ s_2 \end{bmatrix} \tag{8.27}$$

This type of interpolation is called *Hermite interpolation*, after the French mathematician Charles Hermite (1822–1901). Hermite also proved in 1873 that e is transcendental (see page 10).

This interpolant can be used as shown above to blend a pair of numerical values and their tangent vectors, or it can be used to interpolate between points in space. To demonstrate the latter we will explore a 2D example, and it is very easy to implement the technique in 3D.

Figure 8.11 illustrates shows how two points $(0, 0)$ and $(1, 1)$ are to be connected by a cubic curve that responds to the initial and final tangent vectors. At the start point $(0, 1)$ the tangent vector is $[-5 \ 0]^T$, and at the final point $(1, 1)$ the tangent vector is $[0 \ -5]^T$. The x and y interpolants are

$$x = [t^3 \ t^2 \ t^1 \ 1] \cdot \begin{bmatrix} 2 & -2 & 1 & 1 \\ -3 & 3 & -2 & -1 \\ 0 & 0 & 1 & 0 \\ 1 & 0 & 0 & 0 \end{bmatrix} \cdot \begin{bmatrix} 0 \\ 1 \\ -5 \\ 0 \end{bmatrix}$$

$$y = [t^3 \ t^2 \ t^1 \ 1] \cdot \begin{bmatrix} 2 & -2 & 1 & 1 \\ -3 & 3 & -2 & -1 \\ 0 & 0 & 1 & 0 \\ 1 & 0 & 0 & 0 \end{bmatrix} \cdot \begin{bmatrix} 0 \\ 1 \\ 0 \\ -5 \end{bmatrix}$$

which become

$$x = [t^3 \ t^2 \ t^1 \ 1] \cdot \begin{bmatrix} -7 \\ 13 \\ -5 \\ 0 \end{bmatrix} = -7t^3 + 13t^2 - 5t$$

$$y = [t^3 \ t^2 \ t^1 \ 1] \cdot \begin{bmatrix} -7 \\ 8 \\ 0 \\ 0 \end{bmatrix} = -7t^3 + 8t^2$$

When these polynomials are plotted over the range $0 \le t \le 1$, we obtain the curve shown in Figure 8.11.

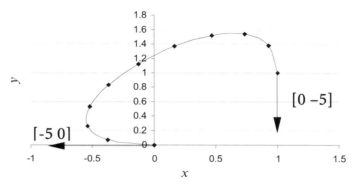

Figure 8.11 *A Hermite curve between the points (0, 0) and (1, 1) with tangent vectors (−5, 0) and (0, −5).*

We have now reached a point where are starting to discover how parametric polynomials can be used to generate space curves, which is the subject of the next chapter. So, to conclude this chapter on interpolants, we will take a look at interpolating vectors.

Interpolating vectors

So far we have been interpolating between a pair of numbers. Now the question arises: can we use the same interpolants for vectors? Perhaps not, because a vector contains both magnitude and direction, and when we interpolate between two vectors we must ensure that both quantities are preserved. For example, if we interpolated the x- and y-components of the vectors $[2\ 3]^T$ and $[4\ 7]^T$, the in-between vectors would preserve the change of orientation but ignore the change in magnitude. To preserve both, we must understand how the interpolation should operate.

Figure 8.12 shows two unit vectors $\mathbf{V}_1$ and $\mathbf{V}_2$ separated by an angle θ. The interpolated vector V can be defined as a proportion of $\mathbf{V}_1$ and a proportion of $\mathbf{V}_2$:

$$\mathbf{V} = a\mathbf{V}_1 + b\mathbf{V}_2 \qquad (8.28)$$

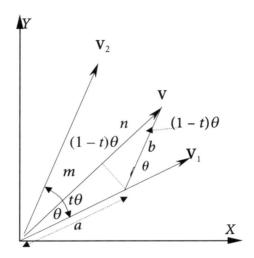

Figure 8.12 *Vector* **V** *is derived from a parts of* **V**$_1$ *and b parts of* **V**$_2$.

Let's define the values of a and b such that they are a function of the separating angle θ. Vector **V** is $t\theta$ from **V**$_1$ and $(1-t)\theta$ from **V**$_2$, and it is evident from Figure 8.12 that using the sine rule

$$\frac{a}{\sin((1-t)\theta)} = \frac{b}{\sin(t\theta)} \qquad (8.29)$$

and furthermore

$$m = a\cos(t\theta) \qquad (8.30)$$

$$n = b\cos((1-t)\theta) \qquad (8.31)$$

$$m + n = 1 \qquad (8.32)$$

From (8.29),

$$b = \frac{a\sin(t\theta)}{\sin((1-t)\theta)} \qquad (8.33)$$

and from (8.32) we get

$$a\cos(t\theta) + \frac{a\sin(t\theta)\cos((1-t)\theta)}{\sin((1-t)\theta)} = 1$$

Solving for a we find

$$a = \frac{\sin((1-t)\theta)}{\sin(\theta)} \quad \text{and} \quad b = \frac{\sin(t\theta)}{\sin(\theta)}$$

Therefore, the final interpolant is

$$\mathbf{V} = \frac{\sin((1-t)\theta)}{\sin(\theta)}\mathbf{V}_1 + \frac{\sin(t\theta)}{\sin(\theta)}\mathbf{V}_2 \tag{8.34}$$

To see how this operates, let's consider a simple exercise of interpolating between two unit vectors $[1 \quad 0]^T$ and $[-\frac{1}{\sqrt{2}} \quad \frac{1}{\sqrt{2}}]^T$. The value of θ is the angle between the two vectors: $135°$. (8.34) is used to interpolate the x-components and the y-components individually:

$$V_x = \frac{\sin((1-t)135°)}{\sin(135°)} \times (1) + \frac{\sin(t135°)}{\sin(135°)} \times (-\frac{1}{\sqrt{2}})$$

$$V_y = \frac{\sin((1-t)135°)}{\sin(135°)} \times (0) + \frac{\sin(t135°)}{\sin(135°)} \times (\frac{1}{\sqrt{2}})$$

Figure 8.13 shows the interpolating curves and Figure 8.14 shows the positions of the interpolated vectors, and a trace of the interpolated vectors.

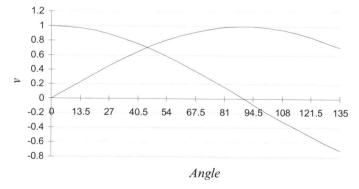

Angle

Figure 8.13 *Curves of the two parts of (8.34).*

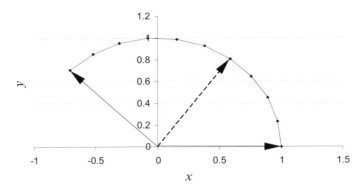

Figure 8.14 *A trace of the interpolated vectors between*
$[1\ 0]^T$ *and* $[-\frac{1}{\sqrt{2}}\ \ \frac{1}{\sqrt{2}}]^T$.

Two observations on (8.34):

- The angle θ is the angle between the two vectors, which, if not known, can be computed using the dot product.
- Secondly, the range of θ is give by $0 \le \theta \le 180°$, because when $\theta = 180°$ the denominator collapses to zero. To confirm this we will repeat (8.34) for $\theta = 179°$. The result is shown in Figure 8.15, which reveals clearly that the interpolant works normally over this range. One more degree, however, and it fails!

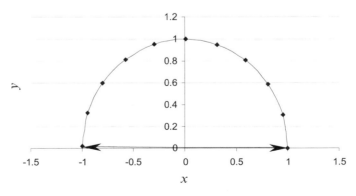

Figure 8.15 *Interpolating between two vectors 179° apart.*

So far, we have only considered unit vectors. Now let's see how the interpolant responds to vectors of different magnitudes. As a test, we can input the following vectors to (8.34):

$$\mathbf{V}_1 = \begin{bmatrix} 2 \\ 0 \end{bmatrix} \quad \text{and} \quad \mathbf{V}_2 = \begin{bmatrix} 0 \\ 1 \end{bmatrix}$$

The separating angle $\theta = 90°$, and the result is shown in Figure 8.16. Note how the initial length of $\mathbf{V}_1$ reduces from 2 to 1 over 90°. It is left to the reader to examine other combinations of vectors. But there is one more application for this interpolant, and that is with quaternions.

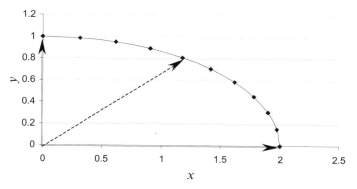

Figure 8.16 *Interpolating between the vectors $[2\ 0]^T$ and $[0\ 1]^T$.*

Interpolating quaternions

It just so happens that the interpolant used for vectors also works with quaternions. Which means that, given two quaternions q_1 and q_2, the interpolated quaternion q is given by

$$\mathbf{q} = \frac{\sin((1-t)\theta)}{\sin(\theta)}\mathbf{q}_1 + \frac{\sin(t\theta)}{\sin(\theta)}\mathbf{q}_2 \tag{8.35}$$

The interpolant is applied individually to the four terms of the quaternion.

When interpolating vectors, θ is the angle between the two vectors. If this is not known, it can be derived using the dot product formula:

$$\cos(\theta) = \frac{\mathbf{V}_1 . \mathbf{V}_2}{|\mathbf{V}_1||\mathbf{V}_2|} \tag{8.36}$$

$$\cos(\theta) = \frac{x_1 x_2 + y_1 y_2 + z_1 z_2}{|\mathbf{V}_1||\mathbf{V}_2|}$$

When interpolating quaternions, θ is discovered by taking the 4D dot product of the two quaternions:

$$\cos(\theta) = \frac{\mathbf{q}_1 . \mathbf{q}_2}{|\mathbf{q}_1||\mathbf{q}_2|}$$

$$\cos(\theta) = \frac{s_1 s_2 + x_1 x_2 + y_1 y_2 + z_1 z_2}{|\mathbf{q}_1||\mathbf{q}_2|}$$

If we are using unit quaternions,

$$\cos(\theta) = s_1 s_2 + x_1 x_2 + y_1 y_2 + z_1 z_2 \tag{8.37}$$

We are now in a position to demonstrate how to interpolate between a pair of quaternions. For example, say we have two quaternions $\mathbf{q}_1$ and $\mathbf{q}_2$ that rotate $0°$ and $90°$ about the z-axis respectively:

$$\mathbf{q}_1 = [\cos(\frac{0°}{2}), \sin(\frac{0°}{2})[0, 0, 1]]$$

$$\mathbf{q}_2 = [\cos(\frac{90°}{2}), \sin(\frac{90°}{2})[0, 0, 1]]$$

which become

$$\mathbf{q}_1 = [1, [0, 0, 0]]$$

$$\mathbf{q}_2 = [0.7071, [0, 0, 0.7071]]$$

Any interpolated quaternion can be found by the application of (8.35). But first, we need to find the value of θ using (8.34):

$$\cos(\theta) = 0.7071 + 0 + 0 + 0$$

$$\theta = 45°$$

Now when $t = 0.5$, the interpolated quaternion is given by

$$q = \frac{\sin(\frac{45°}{2})}{\sin(45°)}[1, [0, 0, 0]] + \frac{\sin(\frac{45°}{2})}{(\sin(45°)}[0.7071, [0, 0, 0.7071]]$$

$$q = 0.541196[1, [0, 0, 0]] + 0.541196[0.7071, [0, 0, 0.7071]]$$

$$q = [0.541196, [0, 0, 0]] + [0.382683, [0, 0, 0.382683]]$$

$$q = [0.923879, [0, 0, 0.382683]]$$

Although it is not obvious, this interpolated quaternion is a unit quaternion, because the square root of the sum of the squares is 1. It should rotate a point about the z-axis, halfway between 0° and 90°, i.e. 45°. We can test that this works with a simple example.

Take a point $(1, 0, 0)$ and subject it to the standard quaternion operation:

$$P' = qPq^{-1}$$

To keep the arithmetic work to a minimum, we substitute $a = 0.923879$ and $b = 0.382683$. Therefore

$$q = [a, [0, 0, b]] \quad \text{and} \quad q^{-1} = [a, [0, 0, -b]]$$

$$P' = [a, [0, 0, b]] \times [0, [1, 0, 0]] \times [a, [0, 0, -b]]$$

$$P' = [0, [a, b, 0]] \times [a, [0, 0, -b]]$$

$$P' = [0, [a^2 - b^2, 2ab, 0]]$$

$$P' = [0, [0.7071, 0.7071, 0]]$$

Therefore, $(1, 0, 0)$ is rotated to $(0.7071, 0.7071, 0)$, which is correct!

Summary

This chapter has covered some very interesting, yet simple ideas about changing one number into another. In the following chapter we will develop these ideas and see how we design algebraic solutions to curves and surfaces.

Chapter 9

Curves and Patches

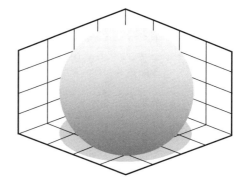

In this chapter we investigate the foundations of curves and surface patches. This is a very large and complex subject, and it is impossible for us to delve too deeply. However, we can explore many of the ideas that are essential to understanding the mathematics behind 2D and 3D curves and how they are developed to produce surface patches. Once you have understood these ideas you will be able to read more advanced texts and develop a wider knowledge.

In the previous chapter we saw how polynomials were used as interpolants and blending functions. We will now see how these can form the basis of parametric curves and patches. To begin with, let's start with the humble circle.

The circle

The circle has a very simple equation:

$$x^2 + y^2 = R^2 \tag{9.1}$$

where R is the radius. Although this equation has its uses, it is not very convenient for drawing the curve. What we really want are two functions that determine the coordinates of any point on the circumference in terms of some parameter. Figure 9.1 shows a scenario where the x- and y-coordinates are given by

$$x = R\cos(t)$$

$$y = R\sin(t) \quad 0 \le t \le 2\pi \tag{9.2}$$

By varying the parameter t over the range 0 to 2π we trace out the curve of the circumference. In fact, by selecting a suitable range of t we can isolate any portion of the circle.

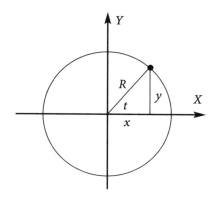

Figure 9.1 *The circle can be drawn by tracing out a series of points on the circumference.*

The ellipse

The equation for an ellipse is

$$\frac{x^2}{R_{maj}^2} + \frac{y^2}{R_{min}^2} \tag{9.3}$$

but its parametric form is

$$x = R_{maj}\cos(t)$$

$$y = R_{min}\sin(t) \quad 0 \le t \le 2\pi \tag{9.4}$$

where R_{maj} and R_{min} are the major and minor radii respectively, as shown in Figure 9.2.

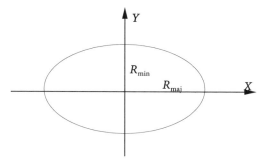

Figure 9.2 *An ellipse showing the major and minor radii..*

In the previous chapter we saw how a Hermite curve could be developed using cubic polynomials and tangent slope vectors. Equation (8.27) gave the x- and y-coordinates for a 2D curve, and there is no reason why it could not be extended to give the z-coordinate for a 3D curve. The tangent slope vectors would also have to be modified to form the end conditions in three dimensions.

We will now examine a very useful parametric curve called a Bézier curve, named after its inventor Pierre Bézier.

Bézier curves

Two people, working for competing French car manufacturers, are associated with what are now called Bézier curves: Paul de Casteljau, who worked at Citroën, and Pierre Bézier, who worked at Rénault. De Casteljau's work was slightly ahead of Bézier, but because of Citroën's policy of secrecy it was never published, so Bézier's name has since been associated with the theory of polynomial curves and surfaces. Casteljau started his research work in 1959, but his reports were only discovered in 1975, by which time Bézier had already become known for his special curves and surfaces.

Bernstein polynomials

Bézier curves employ *Bernstein polynomials*, which were described by S. Bernstein in 1912. They are expressed as follows:

$$B_i^n(t) = \binom{n}{i} t^i (1-t)^{n-i} \qquad (9.5)$$

where $\binom{n}{i}$ is shorthand for the number of selections of i different items from n distinguishable items when the order of selection is ignored, and equals

$$\frac{n!}{(n-i)!i!} \tag{9.6}$$

where, for example, 3! (factorial 3) is shorthand for $3 \times 2 \times 1$.

When (9.6) is evaluated for different values of i and n, we discover the pattern of numbers shown in Table 9.1. This pattern of numbers is known as *Pascal's triangle*. In western countries they are named after a 17th century French mathematician, even though they had been described in China as early as 1303 in *Precious Mirror of the Four Elements* by the Chinese mathematician Chu Shih-chieh. The pattern represents the coefficients found in binomial expansions. For example, the expansion of $(x + a)^n$ for different values of n is

$$(x + a)^0 = 1$$

$$(x + a)^1 = 1x + 1a$$

$$(x + a)^2 = 1x^2 + 2ax + 1a^2$$

$$(x + a)^3 = 1x^3 + 3ax^2 + 3a^2x + 1a^3$$

$$(x + a)^4 = 1x^4 + 4ax^3 + 6a^2x^2 + 4a^3x + 1a^4$$

which reveals Pascal's triangle as coefficients of the polynomial terms.

Table 9.1 *Pascal's triangle*

	i						
n	0	1	2	3	4	5	6
0	1						
1	1	1					
2	1	2	1				
3	1	3	3	1			
4	1	4	6	4	1		
5	1	5	10	10	5	1	
6	1	6	15	20	15	6	1

Pascal, however, recognized other qualities in the numbers, in that they described the odds governing combinations. For example, to determine the probability of any girl–boy combination in a family of 6 children, we sum the numbers in the 6th row of Pascal's triangle:

$$1 + 6 + 15 + 20 + 15 + 6 + 1 = 64.$$

The number (1) at the start and end of the 6th row represent the chances of getting 6 boys or 6 girls, i.e. 1 in 64. The next number (6) represents the next most likely combination: 5 boys and 1 girl, or 5 girls and 1 boy, i.e. 6 in 64. The centre number (20) applies to 3 boys and 3 girls, for which the chances are 20 in 64.

Thus the $\binom{n}{i}$ term in (9.5) is nothing more than a generator for Pascal's triangle. The powers of t and $(1 - t)$ in (9.5) appear as shown in Table 9.2 for different values of n and i. When the two sets of results are combined, we get the complete Bernstein polynomial terms shown in Table 9.3. One very important property of these terms is that they sum to unity, which is an important feature of any interpolant.

Table 9.2 *Expansion of the terms t and (1 − t)*

	i				
n	**0**	**1**	**2**	**3**	**4**
1	t	$(1-t)$			
2	t^2	$t(1-t)$	$(1-t)^2$		
3	t^3	$t^2(1-t)$	$t(1-t)^2$	$(1-t)^3$	
4	t^4	$t^3(1-t)$	$t^2(1-t)^2$	$t(1-t)^3$	$(1-t)^4$

Table 9.3 *The Bernstein polynomial terms*

	i				
n	**0**	**1**	**2**	**3**	**4**
1	$1t$	$1(1-t)$			
2	$1t^2$	$2t(1-t)$	$1(1-t)^2$		
3	$1t^3$	$3t^2(1-t)$	$3t(1-t)^2$	$1(1-t)^3$	
4	$1t^4$	$4t^3(1-t)$	$6t^2(1-t)^2$	$4t(1-t)^3$	$1(1-t)^4$

As the product of $(1 - t)$ and t is 1,

$$((1 - t) + t)^n = 1 \tag{9.7}$$

which is why we can use the binomial expansion of $(1 - t)$ and t as interpolants. When $n = 2$ we obtain the quadratic form

$$(1 - t)^2 \quad 2t(1 - t) \quad t^2 \tag{9.8}$$

Figure 9.3 shows the graphs of the three polynomial terms of (9.8). The $(1 - t)^2$ graph starts at 1 and decays to zero, whereas the t^2 graph starts at zero and rises to 1. The $2t(1 - t)$ graph starts at zero, reaches a maximum of 0.5 and returns to zero. Thus the central polynomial term has no influence at the end-points where $t = 0$ and $t = 1$.

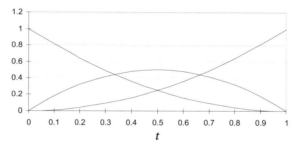

Figure 9.3 *The graphs of the quadratic Bernstein polynomials.*

We can use these three terms to interpolate between a pair of values as follows:

$$V = V_1(1 - t)^2 + 2t(1 - t) + V_2 t^2 \tag{9.9}$$

If $V_1 = 1$ and $V_2 = 3$ we obtain the curve shown in Figure 9.4.

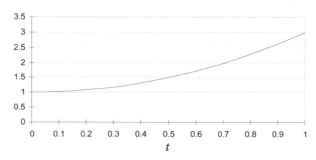

Figure 9.4 *Bernstein interpolation between the values 1 and 3.*

Essential Mathematics for CG *fast*

But there is nothing preventing us from multiplying the middle term $2t(1 - t)$ by any arbitrary number V_c:

$$V = V_1(1 - t)^2 + V_c 2t(1 - t) + V_2 t^2 \qquad (9.10)$$

For example, if $V_c = 3$ we obtain the graph shown in Figure 9.5, which is totally different from Figure 9.4. As Bézier observed, the value of V_c provides an excellent mechanism for determining the shape of the curve between two values. Figure 9.6 shows a variety of graphs for different values of V_c. A very interesting effect occurs when the value of V_c is set midway between V_1 and V_2. For example, when $V_1 = 1$ and $V_2 = 3$ and $V_c = 2$, we obtain linear interpolation between V_1 and V_2, as shown in Figure 9.7.

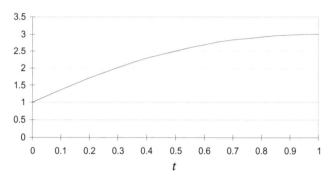

Figure 9.5 *Bernstein interpolation between values 1 and 3 with $V_c = 3$.*

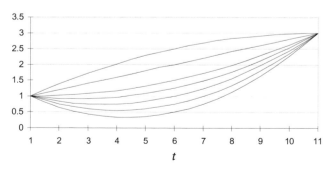

Figure 9.6 *Bernstein interpolation between values 1 and 3 for different values of V_c.*

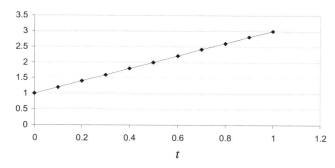

Figure 9.7 *Linear interpolation using a quadratic Bernstein interpolant.*

Quadratic Bézier curves

Quadratic Bézier curves are formed by using Bernstein polynomials to interpolate between the x-, y- and z-coordinates associated with the start- and end-points forming the curve. For example, we can draw a 2D quadratic Bézier curve between $(1, 1)$ and $(4, 3)$ using the following equations:

$$x = 1(1 - t)^2 + x_c 2t(1 - t) + 4t^2$$

$$y = 1(1 - t)^2 + y_c 2t(1 - t) + 3t^2 \qquad (9.11)$$

But what should be the values of (x_c, y_c)? Well, this is entirely up to us. The position of this *control vertex* determines how the curve moves between $(1, 1)$ and $(4, 3)$. A Bézier curve possesses interpolating and approximating qualities: the interpolating feature ensures that the curve passes through the end-points, while the approximating feature shows how the curve passes close to the control point. To illustrate this, if we make $x_c = 3$ and $y_c = 4$ we obtain the curve shown in Figure 9.8, which shows how the curve intersects the end-points, but misses the control point. It also highlights two important features of Bézier curves: the *convex hull* property, and the end slopes of the curve.

The convex hull property implies that the curve is always contained within the polygon connecting the end and control

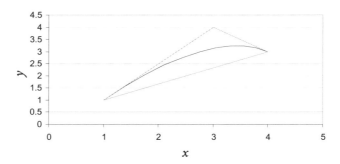

Figure 9.8 *Quadratic Bézier curve between (1, 1) and (4, 3), with (3, 4) as the control vertex..*

points. In this case the curve is inside the triangle formed by the vertices (1, 1), (3, 4) and (4, 3). The slope of the curve at (1, 1) is equal to the slope of the line connecting the start point to the control point (3, 4), and the slope of the curve at (4, 3) is equal to the slope of the line connecting the control point (3, 4) to the end-point (4, 3). Naturally, these two qualities of Bézier curves can be proved mathematically.

Before moving on, there are two further points to note:

- No restrictions are placed on the position of (x_c, y_c) – it can be anywhere.
- Simply including z-coordinates for the start, end and control vertices creates 3D curves.

Cubic Bernstein polynomials

One of the problems with quadratic curves is that they are so simple. If we wanted to construct a complex curve with several peaks and valleys, we would have to join together a large number of such curves. A *cubic curve*, on the other hand, naturally supports one peak and one valley, which simplifies the construction of more complex curves.

When $n = 3$ in (9.7), we obtain the following terms:

$$((1 - t) \; t)^3 = (1 - t)^3 + 3t(1 - t)^2 + 3t^2(1 - t) + t^3 \quad (9.12)$$

which can be used as a cubic interpolant, as

$$V = V_1(1-t)^3 + V_{c1}3t(1-t)^2 + V_{c2}3t^2(1-t) + V_2t^3 \quad (9.13)$$

Once more the terms sum to unity, and the convex hull and slope properties also hold. Figure 9.9 shows the graphs of the four polynomial terms.

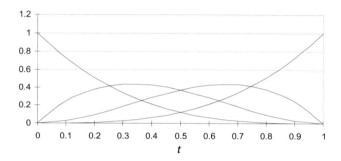

Figure 9.9 *The cubic Bernstein polynomial curves.*

This time we have two control values, V_{c1} and V_{c2}. These can be set to any value, independent of the values chosen for V_1 and V_2. To illustrate this, let's consider an example of blending between values 1 and 3, with V_{c1} and V_{c2} set to 2.5 and -2.5 respectively. The blending curve is shown in Figure 9.10.

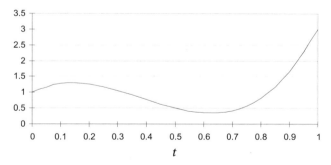

Figure 9.10 *The cubic Bernstein polynomial through the values 1, 2.5, −2.5, 3.*

The next step is to associate the blending polynomials with *x*- and *y*-coordinates:

$$x = x_1(1 - t)^3 + x_{c1}3t(1 - t)^2 + x_{c2}3t^2(1 - t) + x_2t^3$$

$$y = y_1(1 - t)^3 + y_{c1}3t(1 - t)^2 + y_{c2}3t^2(1 - t) + y_2t^3 \qquad (9.14)$$

Evaluating (9.14) with the following points:

$$(x_1, y_1) = (1, 1) \qquad (x_{c1}, y_{c1}) = (2, 3)$$

$$(x_{c2}, y_{c2}) = (3, -2) \qquad (x_2, y_2) = (4, 3)$$

we obtain the cubic Bézier curve as shown in Figure 9.11, which also shows the guidelines between the end and control points.

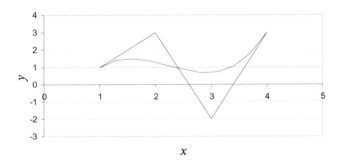

Figure 9.11 *A cubic Bézier curve.*

Just to show how consistent Bernstein polynomials are, let's set the values to

$$(x_1, y_1) = (1, 1) \qquad (x_{c1}, y_{c1}) = (2, 1.666)$$

$$(x_{c2}, y_{c2}) = (3, 2.333) \qquad (x_2, y_2) = (4, 3)$$

where (x_{c1}, y_{c1}) and (x_{c2}, y_{c2}) are points one-third and two-thirds between the start and final values. As we found in the quadratic case, where the single control point was halfway between the start and end values, we obtain linear interpolation as shown in Figure 9.12.

Mathematicians are always interested in finding how to express formulae in compact and precise forms, so they have devised an elegant way of abbreviating (9.11) and (9.14). Equation (9.11) describes the three polynomial terms for generating a quadratic Bézier curve, and (9.14) describes the four polynomial terms for generating a cubic Bézier curve. To

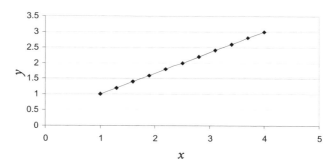

Figure 9.12 *A cubic Bézier line.*

begin with, quadratic equations are called *second-degree equations*, and cubics are called *third-degree equations*. In the original Bernstein formulation,

$$B_i^n(t) = \binom{n}{i} t^i (1-t)^{n-i} \tag{9.15}$$

n represents the degree of the polynomial, and i, which has values between 0 and n, creates the individual polynomial terms. These terms are then used to multiply the coordinates of the end and control points. If these points are stored as a vector $\mathbf{P}$, a point $\mathbf{p}(t)$ on the curve can be written as

$$\mathbf{p}(t) = \binom{n}{i} t^i (1-t)^{n-i} \mathbf{P}_i \text{ for } 0 \le i \le n \tag{9.16}$$

or

$$\mathbf{p}(t) = \sum_{i=0}^{n} \binom{n}{i} t^i (1-t)^{n-i} \mathbf{P}_i \tag{9.17}$$

or

$$\mathbf{p}(t) = \sum_{i=0}^{n} B_i^n(t) \mathbf{P}_i \tag{9.18}$$

For example, a point $\mathbf{p}(t)$ on a quadratic curve is represented by

$$\mathbf{p}(t) = 1t^0(1-t)^2 \mathbf{P}_0 + 2t^1(1-t)^1 \mathbf{P}_1 + 1t^2(1-t)^0 \mathbf{P}_2 \tag{9.19}$$

You will discover (9.17) and (9.18) used in more advanced texts to describe Bézier curves. Although they may initially appear intimidating, you should now find them relatively easy to understand.

A recursive Bézier formula

Note that (9.17) explicitly describes the polynomial terms needed to construct the blending terms. With the use of *recursive functions* (a recursive function is a function that calls itself), it is possible to arrive at another formulation that leads towards an understanding of *B-splines*. To begin, we need to express $\binom{n}{i}$ in terms of lower terms, and because the coefficients of any row in Pascal's triangle are the sum of the two coefficients immediately above, we can write

$$\binom{n}{i} = \binom{n-1}{i} + \binom{n-1}{i-1} \tag{9.20}$$

Therefore, we can write

$$B_i^n(t) = \binom{n-1}{i} t^i (1-t)^{n-i} + \binom{n-1}{i-1} t^i (1-t)^{n-i}$$

$$B_i^n(t) = (1-t) B_i^{n-1}(t) + t B_{i-1}^{n-1}(t) \tag{9.21}$$

As with all recursive functions, some condition must terminate the process: in this case it is when the degree is zero. Consequently, $B_0^0(t) \equiv 1$ and $B_j^n(t) \equiv 0$ for $j < 0$.

Bézier curves using matrices

As we have already seen, matrices provide a very compact notation for algebraic formulae. So let's see how Bernstein polynomials lend themselves to this form of notation. Recall (9.11), which defines the three terms associated with a quadratic Bernstein polynomial. These can be expanded to

$$(1 - 2t + t^2) \quad (2t - 2t^2) \quad (t^2) \tag{9.22}$$

and can be written as the product of two matrices:

$$[t^2 \ t \ 1] \cdot \begin{bmatrix} 1 & -2 & 1 \\ -2 & 2 & 0 \\ 1 & 0 & 0 \end{bmatrix} \tag{9.23}$$

This means that (9.13) can be expressed as

$$V = [t^2 \ t \ 1] \cdot \begin{bmatrix} 1 & -2 & 1 \\ -2 & 2 & 0 \\ 1 & 0 & 0 \end{bmatrix} \cdot \begin{bmatrix} V_1 \\ V_c \\ V_2 \end{bmatrix} \tag{9.24}$$

and (9.14) as

$$\mathbf{p}(t) = [t^2 \ t \ 1] \cdot \begin{bmatrix} 1 & -2 & 1 \\ -2 & 2 & 0 \\ 1 & 0 & 0 \end{bmatrix} \cdot \begin{bmatrix} \mathbf{P}_1 \\ \mathbf{P}_c \\ \mathbf{P}_2 \end{bmatrix} \tag{9.25}$$

where $\mathbf{p}(t)$ is any point on the curve, and $\mathbf{P}_1$, $\mathbf{P}_c$ and $\mathbf{P}_2$ are the start, control and end-points respectively.

A similar development can be used for a cubic Bézier curve, which has the following matrix formulation:

$$\mathbf{p}(t) = [t^3 \ t^2 \ t \ 1] \cdot \begin{bmatrix} -1 & 3 & -3 & 1 \\ 3 & -6 & 3 & 0 \\ -3 & 3 & 0 & 0 \\ 1 & 0 & 0 & 0 \end{bmatrix} \cdot \begin{bmatrix} \mathbf{P}_1 \\ \mathbf{P}_{c1} \\ \mathbf{P}_{c2} \\ \mathbf{P}_2 \end{bmatrix} \tag{9.26}$$

There is no doubt that Bézier curves are very useful, and they find their way into all sorts of applications. Perhaps their one weakness, however, is that whenever an end or control vertex is repositioned, the entire curve is modified. So let's examine another type of curve that prevents this from happening: B-splines. But before we consider their cubic form, let's revisit linear interpolation between multiple values.

Linear interpolation

To interpolate linearly between two values V_0 and V_1, we use the following interpolant:

$$V(t) = V_0(1 - t) + V_1 t \quad \text{for } 0 \le t \le 1 \tag{9.27}$$

But say we have to interpolate continuously between three values on a linear basis, i.e. V_0, V_1, V_2, with the possibility of extending the technique to any number of values. One solution is to use a sequence of parameter values t_1, t_2, t_3 that are associated with the given values of V, as shown in Figure 9.13. For the sake of symmetry V_0 is associated with the parameter range t_0 to t_2, V_1 is associated with the parameter range t_1 to t_3, and V_2 is associated with the parameter range t_2 to t_4. This sequence of parameters is called a *knot vector*. The only assumption we make about the knot vector is that $t_0 \le t_1 \le t_2 \le$, etc.

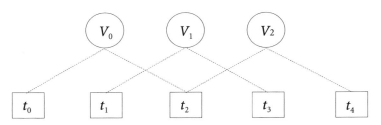

Figure 9.13 *Linearly interpolating between several values.*

Now let's invent a linear blending function $B_i^1(t)$ whose subscript i is used to reference values in the knot vector. We want to use the blending function to compute the influence of the three values on any interpolated value $V(t)$ as follows:

$$V(t) = B_0^1(t)V_0 + B_1^1(t)V_1 + B_2^1(t)V_2 \tag{9.28}$$

It's obvious from this arrangement that V_0 will influence $V(t)$ only when t is between t_0 and t_2. Similarly, V_1 and V_2 will influence $V(t)$ only when t is between t_1 and t_3, and t_2 and t_4 respectively.

To understand the action of the blending function let's concentrate on one particular value $B_1^1(t)$. When t is less than t_1 or greater than t_3, the function $B_1^1(t)$ must be zero. When $t_1 \leq t \leq t_3$, the function must return a value reflecting the proportion of V_1 that influences $V(t)$. During the span $t_1 \leq t \leq t_2$, V_1 has to be blended in, and during the span $t_1 \leq t \leq t_3$, V_1 has to be blended out. The blending in is effected by the ratio

$$\left(\frac{t - t_1}{t_2 - t_1} \right) \tag{9.29}$$

and the blending out is effected by the ratio

$$\left(\frac{t_3 - t}{t_3 - t_2} \right) \tag{9.30}$$

Thus $B_1^1(t)$ has to incorporate both ratios, but it must ensure that they only become active during the appropriate range of t. Let's remind ourselves of this requirement by subscripting the ratios accordingly:

$$B_1^1(t) = \left(\frac{t - t_1}{t_2 - t_1} \right)_{1,2} + \left(\frac{t_3 - t}{t_3 - t_2} \right)_{2,3} \tag{9.31}$$

We can now write the other two blending terms $B_0^1(t)$ and $B_2^1(t)$ as

$$B_0^1(t) = \left(\frac{t - t_0}{t_1 - t_0} \right)_{0,1} + \left(\frac{t_2 - t}{t_2 - t_1} \right)_{1,2} \tag{9.32}$$

$$B_2^1(t) = \left(\frac{t - t_2}{t_3 - t_2} \right)_{2,3} + \left(\frac{t_4 - t}{t_4 - t_3} \right)_{3,4} \tag{9.33}$$

You should be able to see a pattern linking the variables with their subscripts, and the possibility of writing a general linear blending term $B_i^1(t)$ as

$$B_i^1(t) = \left(\frac{t - t_i}{t_{i+1} - t_i} \right)_{i,i+1} + \left(\frac{t_{i+2} - t}{t_{i+2} - t_{i+1}} \right)_{i+1,i+2} \tag{9.34}$$

This enables us to write (9.28) in a general form as

$$V(t) = \sum_{i=0}^{2} B_i^1(t) V_i \tag{9.35}$$

But there is still a problem concerning the values associated with the knot vector. Fortunately, there is an easy solution. One simple approach is to keep the differences between t_1, t_2 and t_3 whole numbers, e.g. 0, 1 and 2. But what about the end conditions t_0 and t_4? To understand the resolution of this problem, let's examine the action of the three terms over the range of the parameter t. The three terms are

$$\left[\left(\frac{t-t_0}{t_1-t_0}\right)_{0,1} + \left(\frac{t_2-t}{t_2-t_1}\right)_{1,2}\right]V_0 \tag{9.36}$$

$$\left[\left(\frac{t-t_1}{t_2-t_1}\right)_{1,2} + \left(\frac{t_3-t}{t_3-t_2}\right)_{2,3}\right]V_1 \tag{9.37}$$

$$\left[\left(\frac{t-t_2}{t_3-t_2}\right)_{2,3} + \left(\frac{t_4-t}{t_4-t_3}\right)_{3,4}\right]V_2 \tag{9.38}$$

and I propose that the knot vector be initialized with the following values:

t_0	t_1	t_2	t_3	t_4
0	0	1	2	2

- Remember that the subscripts of the ratios are the subscripts of t, not the values of t.
- Over the range $t_0 \leq t \leq t_1$, i.e. 0 to 0. Only the first ratio in (9.36) is active and returns $\frac{0}{0}$. The algorithm must detect this condition and take no action.
- Over the range $t_1 \leq t \leq t_2$, i.e. 0 to 1. The first ratio of (9.36) is active again, and over the range of t blends out V_0. The first ratio of (9.37) is also active, and over the range of t blends in V_1.
- Over the range $t_2 \leq t \leq t_3$, i.e. 1 to 2. The second ratio of (9.37) is active, and over the range of t blends out V_1. The first ratio of (9.38) is also active, and over the range of t blends in V_2.
- Finally, over the range $t_3 \leq t \leq t_4$, i.e. 2 to 2. The second ratio of (9.38) is active and returns $\frac{0}{0}$. Once more, the algorithm must detect this condition and take no action.

This process results in a linear interpolation between V_0, V_1 and V_2. If (9.36), (9.37) and (9.38) are applied to coordinate values, the result is two straight lines. This seems like a lot of work just to draw two lines, but the beauty of the technique is that it will work with any number of points, and can be developed for quadratic and higher interpolations.

A. Aitken developed the following recursive interpolant:

$$\mathbf{p}_i^r(t) = \frac{t_{i+r} - t}{t_{i+r} - t_i} \mathbf{p}_i^{r-1}(t) + \frac{t - t_i}{t_{i+r} - t_i} \mathbf{p}_{i+1}^{r-1}(t);$$

$$\begin{cases} r = 1,..n; \\ i = 0,..n-r; \end{cases}$$

(9.39)

which interpolates between a series of points using repeated linear interpolation.

B-splines

B-splines, like Bézier curves, use polynomials to generate a curve segment. But, unlike Bézier curves, B-splines employ a series of control points that determine the curve's local geometry. This feature ensures that only a small portion of the curve is changed when a control point is moved.

There are two types of B-splines: *rational* and *non-rational* splines, which divide into two further categories: *uniform* and *non-uniform*. Rational B-splines are formed from the ratio of two polynomials such as

$$x(t) = \frac{X(t)}{W(t)}, \quad y(t) = \frac{Y(t)}{W(t)}, \quad z(t) = \frac{Z(t)}{W(t)},$$

Although this appears to introduce an unnecessary complication, the division by a second polynomial brings certain advantages:

• They describe perfect circles, ellipses, parabolas and hyperbolas, whereas non-rational curves can only approximate these curves.

- They are invariant of their control points when subjected to rotation, scaling, translation and perspective transformations, whereas non-rational curves lose this geometric integrity.
- They allow weights to be used at the control points to push and pull the curve.

An explanation of uniform and non-uniform types is best left until you understand the idea of splines. So, without knowing the meaning of uniform, let's begin with uniform B-splines.

Uniform B-splines

A B-spline is constructed from a string of curve segments whose geometry is determined by a group of local control points. These curves are known as *piecewise polynomials.* A curve segment does not have to pass through a control point, although this may be desirable at the two end-points.

Cubic B-splines are very common, as they provide a geometry that is one step away from simple quadratics, and possess continuity characteristics that make the joins between the segments invisible. In order to understand their construction, consider the scenario in Figure 9.14. Here we see a group of $(m + 1)$ control points $P_0, P_1, P_2, \ldots, P_m$ which determine the shape of a cubic curve constructed from a series of curve segments $S_0, S_1, S_2, \ldots, S_{m-3}$.

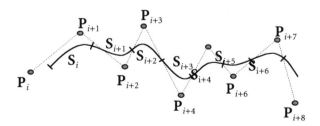

Figure 9.14 *The construction of a uniform non-rational B-spline curve.*

As the curve is cubic, curve segment S_i is influenced by P_i, P_{i+1}, P_{i+2}, P_{i+3}, and curve segment S_{i+1} is influenced by P_{i+1}, P_{i+2}, P_{i+3}, P_{i+4}. There are $(m + 1)$ control points, so there are $(m - 2)$ curve segments.

A single segment $S_i(t)$ of a B-spline curve is defined by

$$S_i(t) = \sum_{r=0}^{3} P_{i+r} B_r(t) \quad for \quad 0 \le t \le 1 \tag{9.40}$$

where

$$B_0(t) = \frac{-t^3 + 3t^2 - 3t + 1}{6} = \frac{(1-t)^3}{6} \tag{9.41}$$

$$B_1(t) = \frac{3t^3 - 6t^2 + 4}{6} \tag{9.42}$$

$$B_2(t) = \frac{-3t^3 + 3t^2 + 3t + 1}{6} \tag{9.43}$$

$$B_3(t) = \frac{t^3}{6} \tag{9.44}$$

These are the B-spline *basis functions* and are shown in Figure 9.15.

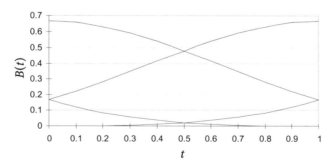

Figure 9.15 The B-spline basis functions.

Although it is not apparent, these four curve segments are part of one curve. The basis function B_3 starts at zero and rises to 0.1666 at $t = 1$. It is taken over by B_2 at $t = 0$, which rises to 0.666 at $t = 1$. The next segment is B_1, which takes over at $t = 0$ and falls to 0.1666 at $t = 1$. Finally, B_0 takes over at 0.1666 and falls to zero at $t = 1$. Equations (9.28) − (9.31) are represented in matrix form by

$$\mathbf{Q}_1(t) = [t^3 \; t^2 \; t \; 1] \cdot \frac{1}{6} \cdot \begin{bmatrix} -1 & 3 & -3 & 1 \\ 3 & -6 & 3 & 0 \\ -3 & 0 & 3 & 0 \\ 1 & 4 & 1 & 0 \end{bmatrix} \begin{bmatrix} P_i \\ P_{i+1} \\ P_{i+2} \\ P_{i+3} \end{bmatrix} \tag{9.45}$$

Let's now illustrate how (9.45) works. We first identify the control points P_i, P_{i+1}, P_{i+2}, etc. Let these be $(0, 1), (1, 3), (2, 0)$, $(4, 1), (4, 3), (2, 2)$ and $(2, 3)$. They can be seen in Figure 9.16 connected together by straight lines. If we take the first four control points: $(0, 1), (1, 3), (2, 0), (4, 1)$, and subject the x- and y-coordinates to the matrix in (9.45) over the range $0 \le t \le 1$, we obtain the first B-spline curve segment shown in Figure 9.16. If we move along one control point and take the next group of control points $(1, 3), (2, 0), (4, 1), (4, 3)$, we obtain the second B-spline curve segment. This is repeated a further two times.

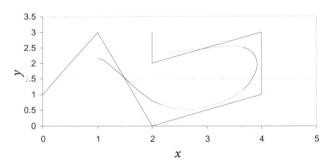

Figure 9.16 *Four curve segments forming a B-spline curve.*

Figure 9.16 shows the four curve segments using two gray scales, and it is obvious that even though there are four discrete segments, they join together perfectly. This is no accident. The slopes at the end-points of the basis curves are designed to match the slopes of their neighbours and ultimately to keep the geometric curve continuous.

Continuity

Constructing curves from several segments can only succeed if the slopes of the abutting curves match. As we are dealing with curves whose slopes are changing everywhere, it is necessary to ensure that even the rate of change of slopes is matched at the join. This aspect of curve design is called *geometric continuity* and is determined by the continuity properties of the basis function. Let's explore such features.

The *first level* of curve continuity, C^0, ensures that the physical end of one basis curve corresponds with the following, e.g. $S_i(1) = S_{i+1}(0)$. We know that this occurs by the graphs shown in Figure 9.15. The *second level* of curve continuity, C^1, ensures that the slope at the end of one basis curve matches that of the following curve. This can be confirmed by differentiating the basis functions (9.28) $-$ (9.31):

$$\mathbf{B}'_0(t) = \frac{-3t^2 + 6t - 3}{6} \tag{9.46}$$

$$\mathbf{B}'_1(t) = \frac{9t^2 - 12t}{6} \tag{9.47}$$

$$\mathbf{B}'_2(t) = \frac{-9t^2 + 6t + 3}{6} \tag{9.48}$$

$$\mathbf{B}'_3(t) = \frac{3t^2}{6} \tag{9.49}$$

Evaluating (9.46) $-$ (9.49) for $t = 0$ and $t = 1$, we discover the slopes $0.5, 0, -0.5, 0$ for the joins between $\mathbf{B}_3, \mathbf{B}_2, \mathbf{B}_1, \mathbf{B}_0$. The *third level* of curve continuity, C^2, ensures that the rate of change of slope at the end of one basis curve matches that of the following curve. This can be confirmed by differentiating (9.46) $-$ (9.49):

$$\mathbf{B}''_0(t) = -t + 1 \tag{9.50}$$

$$\mathbf{B}''_1(t) = 3t - 2 \tag{9.51}$$

$$\mathbf{B}''_2(t) = -3t + 1 \tag{9.52}$$

$$\mathbf{B}''_3(t) = t \tag{9.53}$$

Evaluating (9.50) $-$ (9.53) for $t = 0$ and $t = 1$, we discover the values 1, -2, 1, 0 for the joins between $\mathbf{B}_3$, $\mathbf{B}_2$, $\mathbf{B}_1$, $\mathbf{B}_0$. These combined continuity results are tabulated in Table 9.4.

Table 9.4 Continuity properties of cubic B-splines

C^0	t		C^1	t		C^2	t	
	0	1		0	1		0	1
$B_3(t)$	0	1/6	$B_3'(t)$	0	0.5	$B_3''(t)$	0	1
$B_2(t)$	1/6	2/3	$B_2'(t)$	0.5	0	$B_2''(t)$	1	-2
$B_1(t)$	2/3	1/6	$B_1'(t)$	0	-0.5	$B_1''(t)$	-2	1
$B_0(t)$	1/6	0	$B_0'(t)$	-0.5	0	$B_0''(t)$	1	0

Non-uniform B-splines

Uniform B-splines are constructed from curve segments where the parameter spacing is at equal intervals. *Non-uniform* B-splines, with the support of a knot vector, provide extra shape control and the possibility of drawing periodic shapes. Unfortunately an explanation of the underlying mathematics would take us beyond the introductory nature of this text, and readers are advised to seek out other books dealing in such matters.

Non-uniform rational B-splines

Non-uniform rational B-splines (NURBS) combine the advantages of non-uniform B-splines and rational polynomials: they support periodic shapes such as circles, and they accurately describe curves associated with the conic sections. They also play a very important role in describing geometry used in the modelling of computer animation characters.

NURBS surfaces also have a patch formulation and play a very important role in surface modelling in computer animation and CAD. However, tempting though it is to give a description of NURBS surfaces here, they have been omitted because their inclusion would unbalance the introductory nature of this text.

Surface patches

Planar surface patch

The simplest form of surface geometry consists of a patchwork of polygons or triangles, where three or more vertices provide the basis for describing the associated planar surface. For example, given four vertices P_{00}, P_{10}, P_{01}, P_{11}, as shown in Figure 9.17, a point P_{uv} can be defined as follows. To begin with, a point along the edge $P_{00} - P_{10}$ is defined as

$$P_{u1} = (1 - u)P_{00} + uP_{10} \tag{9.54}$$

and a point along the edge $P_{01} - P_{11}$ is defined as

$$P_{u2} = (1 - u)P_{01} + uP_{11} \tag{9.55}$$

Therefore, any point P_{uv} is defined as

$$P_{uv} = (1 - v)P_{u1} + vP_{u2}$$

$$P_{uv} = (1 - v)[(1 - u)P_{00} + uP_{10}] + v[(1 - u)P_{01} + uP_{11}]$$

$$P_{uv} = (1 - u)(1 - v)P_{00} + u(1 - v)P_{10} + v(1 - u)P_{01} + uvP_{11} \tag{9.56}$$

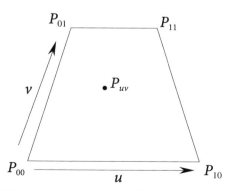

Figure 9.17 *A flat patch defined by u and v parameters.*

This, however, can be written in matrix form as

$$P_{uv} = [(1 - u) \; u] \cdot \begin{bmatrix} P_{00} & P_{01} \\ P_{10} & P_{11} \end{bmatrix} \cdot \begin{bmatrix} (1-v) \\ v \end{bmatrix} \tag{9.57}$$

which expands to

$$P_{uv} = [u \; 1] \cdot \begin{bmatrix} -1 & 1 \\ 1 & 0 \end{bmatrix} \cdot \begin{bmatrix} P_{00} & P_{01} \\ P_{10} & P_{11} \end{bmatrix} \cdot \begin{bmatrix} -1 & 1 \\ 1 & 0 \end{bmatrix} \cdot \begin{bmatrix} v \\ 1 \end{bmatrix} \tag{9.58}$$

Let's illustrate this with an example. Given the following four points: $P_{00} = (0,0,0), P_{10} = (0,0,4) \; P_{01} = (2,2,1), P_{11} = (2,2,3)$, we can write the coordinates of any point on the patch as

$$x_{uv} = [u \; 1] \cdot \begin{bmatrix} -1 & 1 \\ 1 & 0 \end{bmatrix} \cdot \begin{bmatrix} 0 & 2 \\ 0 & 2 \end{bmatrix} \cdot \begin{bmatrix} -1 & 1 \\ 1 & 0 \end{bmatrix} \cdot \begin{bmatrix} v \\ 1 \end{bmatrix}$$

$$y_{uv} = [u \; 1] \cdot \begin{bmatrix} -1 & 1 \\ 1 & 0 \end{bmatrix} \cdot \begin{bmatrix} 0 & 2 \\ 0 & 2 \end{bmatrix} \cdot \begin{bmatrix} -1 & 1 \\ 1 & 0 \end{bmatrix} \cdot \begin{bmatrix} v \\ 1 \end{bmatrix}$$

$$z_{uv} = [u \; 1] \cdot \begin{bmatrix} -1 & 1 \\ 1 & 0 \end{bmatrix} \cdot \begin{bmatrix} 0 & 1 \\ 4 & 3 \end{bmatrix} \cdot \begin{bmatrix} -1 & 1 \\ 1 & 0 \end{bmatrix} \cdot \begin{bmatrix} v \\ 1 \end{bmatrix}$$

$$x_{uv} = 2v$$

$$y_{uv} = 2v$$

$$z_{uv} = u(4 - 2v) + v$$

By substituting values of u and v in (9.47) between the range $0 \le u, v \le 1$ we obtain the coordinates of any point on the surface of the patch.

If we now introduce the ideas of Bézier control points into a surface patch definition, we provide a very powerful way of creating smooth 3D surface patches.

Quadratic Bézier surface patch

Bézier proposed a matrix of nine control points to determine the geometry of a quadratic patch, as shown in Figure 9.18. Any point on the patch is defined by

$$P_{uv} = [u^2 \; u \; 1] \cdot \begin{bmatrix} 1 & -2 & 1 \\ -2 & 2 & 0 \\ 1 & 0 & 0 \end{bmatrix} \cdot \begin{bmatrix} P_{00} & P_{01} & P_{02} \\ P_{10} & P_{11} & P_{12} \\ P_{20} & P_{21} & P_{22} \end{bmatrix} \cdot$$

$$\begin{bmatrix} 1 & -2 & 1 \\ -2 & 2 & 0 \\ 1 & 0 & 0 \end{bmatrix} \cdot \begin{bmatrix} v^2 \\ v \\ 1 \end{bmatrix}$$

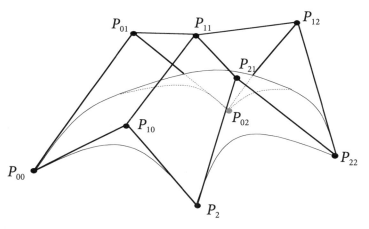

Figure 9.18 *A quadratic Bézier surface patch.*

The individual x, y and z-coordinates are obtained by substituting the x, y and z values for the central P matrix.

Let's illustrate the process with an example. Given the following points:

$P_{00} = (0, 0, 0)$	$P_{01} = (1, 1, 0)$	$P_{02} = (2, 0, 0)$
$P_{10} = (0, 1, 1)$	$P_{11} = (1, 2, 1)$	$P_{12} = (2, 1, 1)$
$P_{20} = (0, 0, 2)$	$P_{21} = (1, 1, 2)$	$P_{22} = (2, 0, 2)$

we can write

$$x_{uv} = [u^2 \ u \ 1] \cdot \begin{bmatrix} 1 & -2 & 1 \\ -2 & 2 & 0 \\ 1 & 0 & 0 \end{bmatrix} \cdot \begin{bmatrix} 0 & 1 & 2 \\ 0 & 1 & 2 \\ 0 & 1 & 2 \end{bmatrix} \cdot$$

$$\begin{bmatrix} 1 & -2 & 1 \\ -2 & 2 & 0 \\ 1 & 0 & 0 \end{bmatrix} \cdot \begin{bmatrix} v^2 \\ v \\ 1 \end{bmatrix}$$

$$x_{uv} = [u^2 \ u \ 1] \cdot \begin{bmatrix} 0 & 0 & 0 \\ 0 & 0 & 0 \\ 0 & 2 & 0 \end{bmatrix} \cdot \begin{bmatrix} v^2 \\ v \\ 1 \end{bmatrix}$$

$$x_{uv} = 2v$$

$$y_{uv} = [u^2 \ u \ 1] \cdot \begin{bmatrix} 1 & -2 & 1 \\ -2 & 2 & 0 \\ 1 & 0 & 0 \end{bmatrix} \cdot \begin{bmatrix} 0 & 1 & 0 \\ 1 & 2 & 1 \\ 0 & 1 & 0 \end{bmatrix} \cdot$$

$$\begin{bmatrix} 1 & -2 & 1 \\ -2 & 2 & 0 \\ 1 & 0 & 0 \end{bmatrix} \cdot \begin{bmatrix} v^2 \\ v \\ 1 \end{bmatrix}$$

$$y_{uv} = [u^2 \ u \ 1] \cdot \begin{bmatrix} 0 & 0 & -2 \\ 0 & 0 & 2 \\ -2 & 2 & 0 \end{bmatrix} \cdot \begin{bmatrix} v^2 \\ v \\ 1 \end{bmatrix}$$

$$y_{uv} = 2(u + v - u^2 - v^2)$$

$$z_{uv} = [u^2 \ u \ 1] \cdot \begin{bmatrix} 1 & -2 & 1 \\ -2 & 2 & 0 \\ 1 & 0 & 0 \end{bmatrix} \cdot \begin{bmatrix} 0 & 0 & 0 \\ 1 & 1 & 1 \\ 2 & 2 & 2 \end{bmatrix} \cdot$$

$$\begin{bmatrix} 1 & -2 & 1 \\ -2 & 2 & 0 \\ 1 & 0 & 0 \end{bmatrix} \cdot \begin{bmatrix} v^2 \\ v \\ 1 \end{bmatrix}$$

$$z_{uv} = [u^2 \ u \ 1] \cdot \begin{bmatrix} 0 & 0 & 0 \\ 0 & 0 & 2 \\ 0 & 0 & 0 \end{bmatrix} \cdot \begin{bmatrix} v^2 \\ v \\ 1 \end{bmatrix}$$

$$z_{uv} = 2u$$

Therefore, any point on the surface patch has coordinates

$$x_{uv} = 2v, \ y_{uv} = 2(u + v - u^2 - v^2), \ z_{uv} = 2u$$

Table 9.5 shows the coordinate values for different values of u and v. In this example, the y-coordinates provide the surface curvature, which could be enhanced by modifying the y-coordinates of the control points.

Table 9.5 The x, y, z coordinates for different values of u and v

		v		
		0	$\frac{1}{2}$	**1**
	0	$(0,0,0)$	$(1,\frac{1}{2},0)$	$(2,0,0)$
u	$\frac{1}{2}$	$(0,\frac{1}{2},1)$	$(1,\frac{1}{2},1)$	$(2,\frac{1}{2},1)$
	1	$(0,0,2)$	$(1,\frac{1}{2},2)$	$(2,0,2)$

Cubic Bézier surface patch

As we saw earlier in this chapter, cubic Bézier curves require two end-points, and two central control points. In the surface patch formulation a 4 × 4 matrix is required as follows:

$$P_{uv} = [u^3 \ u^2 \ u \ 1] \cdot \begin{bmatrix} -1 & 3 & -3 & 1 \\ 3 & -6 & 3 & 0 \\ -3 & 3 & 0 & 0 \\ 1 & 0 & 0 & 0 \end{bmatrix} \begin{bmatrix} P_{00} & P_{01} & P_{02} & P_{03} \\ P_{10} & P_{11} & P_{12} & P_{13} \\ P_{20} & P_{21} & P_{22} & P_{23} \\ P_{30} & P_{31} & P_{32} & P_{33} \end{bmatrix} \cdot$$

$$\begin{bmatrix} -1 & 3 & -3 & 1 \\ 3 & -6 & 3 & 0 \\ -3 & 3 & 0 & 0 \\ 1 & 0 & 0 & 0 \end{bmatrix} \cdot \begin{bmatrix} v^3 \\ v^2 \\ v \\ 1 \end{bmatrix}$$

which can be illustrated by an example.

Given the points:

$$P_{00} = (0,0,0) \quad P_{01} = (1,1,0) \quad P_{02} = (2,1,0) \quad P_{03} = (3,0,0)$$
$$P_{10} = (0,1,1) \quad P_{11} = (1,2,1) \quad P_{12} = (2,2,1) \quad P_{13} = (3,1,1)$$
$$P_{20} = (0,1,2) \quad P_{21} = (1,2,2) \quad P_{22} = (2,2,2) \quad P_{23} = (3,1,2)$$
$$P_{30} = (0,0,3) \quad P_{31} = (1,1,3) \quad P_{32} = (2,1,3) \quad P_{33} = (3,0,3)$$

we can write the following matrix equations:

$$x_{uv} = [u^3 \; u^2 \; u \; 1] \cdot \begin{bmatrix} -1 & 3 & -3 & 1 \\ 3 & -6 & 3 & 0 \\ -3 & 3 & 0 & 0 \\ 1 & 0 & 0 & 0 \end{bmatrix} \cdot \begin{bmatrix} 0 & 1 & 2 & 3 \\ 0 & 1 & 2 & 3 \\ 0 & 1 & 2 & 3 \\ 0 & 1 & 2 & 3 \end{bmatrix} \cdot$$

$$\begin{bmatrix} -1 & 3 & -3 & 1 \\ 3 & -6 & 3 & 0 \\ -3 & 3 & 0 & 0 \\ 1 & 0 & 0 & 0 \end{bmatrix} \cdot \begin{bmatrix} v^3 \\ v^2 \\ v \\ 1 \end{bmatrix}$$

$$x_{uv} = [u^3 \; u^2 \; u \; 1] \cdot \begin{bmatrix} 0 & 0 & 0 & 0 \\ 0 & 0 & 0 & 0 \\ 0 & 0 & 0 & 0 \\ 0 & 0 & 3 & 0 \end{bmatrix} \cdot \begin{bmatrix} v^3 \\ v^2 \\ v \\ 1 \end{bmatrix}$$

$$x_{uv} = 3u$$

$$y_{uv} = [u^3 \; u^2 \; u \; 1] \cdot \begin{bmatrix} -1 & 3 & -3 & 1 \\ 3 & -6 & 3 & 0 \\ -3 & 3 & 0 & 0 \\ 1 & 0 & 0 & 0 \end{bmatrix} \cdot \begin{bmatrix} 0 & 1 & 1 & 0 \\ 1 & 2 & 2 & 1 \\ 1 & 2 & 2 & 1 \\ 0 & 1 & 1 & 0 \end{bmatrix} \cdot$$

$$\begin{bmatrix} -1 & 3 & -3 & 1 \\ 3 & -6 & 3 & 0 \\ -3 & 3 & 0 & 0 \\ 1 & 0 & 0 & 0 \end{bmatrix} \cdot \begin{bmatrix} v^3 \\ v^2 \\ v \\ 1 \end{bmatrix}$$

$$y_{uv} = [u^3 \ u^2 \ u \ 1] \cdot \begin{bmatrix} 0 & 0 & 0 & 0 \\ 0 & 0 & 0 & -3 \\ 0 & 0 & 0 & 3 \\ 0 & -3 & 3 & 0 \end{bmatrix} \cdot \begin{bmatrix} v^3 \\ v^2 \\ v \\ 1 \end{bmatrix}$$

$$y_{uv} = 3(u + v - u^2 - v^2)$$

$$z_{uv} = [u^3 \ u^2 \ u \ 1] \cdot \begin{bmatrix} -1 & 3 & -3 & 1 \\ 3 & -6 & 3 & 0 \\ -3 & 3 & 0 & 0 \\ 1 & 0 & 0 & 0 \end{bmatrix} \cdot \begin{bmatrix} 0 & 0 & 0 & 0 \\ 1 & 1 & 1 & 1 \\ 2 & 2 & 2 & 2 \\ 3 & 3 & 3 & 3 \end{bmatrix} \cdot$$

$$\begin{bmatrix} -1 & 3 & -3 & 1 \\ 3 & -6 & 3 & 0 \\ -3 & 3 & 0 & 0 \\ 1 & 0 & 0 & 0 \end{bmatrix} \cdot \begin{bmatrix} v^3 \\ v^2 \\ v \\ 1 \end{bmatrix}$$

$$z_{uv} = [u^3 \ u^2 \ u \ 1] \cdot \begin{bmatrix} 0 & 0 & 0 & 0 \\ 0 & 0 & 0 & 0 \\ 0 & 0 & 0 & 3 \\ 0 & 0 & 0 & 0 \end{bmatrix} \cdot \begin{bmatrix} v^3 \\ v^2 \\ v \\ 1 \end{bmatrix}$$

$$z_{uv} = 3u$$

Therefore, any point on the surface patch has coordinates

$$x_{uv} = 3v, \ y_{uv} = 3(u + v - u^2 - v^2), \ z_{uv} = 3u$$

Table 9.6 shows the coordinate values for different values of u and v. In this example, the y-coordinates provide the surface curvature, which could be enhanced by modifying the y-coordinates of the control points.

Table 9.6 The x, y, z coordinates for different values of u and v

		v		
		0	$\frac{1}{2}$	1
	0	$(0,0,0)$	$(1\frac{1}{2},\frac{3}{4},0)$	$(3,0,0)$
u	$\frac{1}{2}$	$(0,\frac{3}{4},1\frac{1}{2})$	$(1\frac{1}{2},1\frac{1}{2},1\frac{1}{2})$	$(3,\frac{3}{4},1\frac{1}{2})$
	1	$(0,0,3)$	$(1\frac{1}{2},\frac{3}{4},3)$	$(3,0,3)$

Complex 3D surfaces are readily modelled using Bézier patches. One simply creates a mesh of patches such that their control points are shared at the joins. Surface continuity is controlled using the same mechanism for curves. But where the slopes of trailing and starting control edges apply for curves, the corresponding slopes of control tiles apply for patches.

Summary

This chapter has been the most challenging one to write. On the one hand, the subject is vital to every aspect of computer graphics, but on the other, the reader is required to wrestle with cubic polynomials and a little calculus. However, I do hope that I have managed to communicate some essential concepts behind curves and surfaces, and that you will be tempted to implement some of the mathematics.

Chapter

10

Analytic Geometry

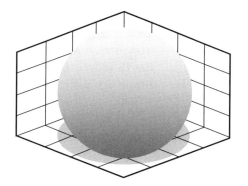

This chapter explores some basic elements of geometry and analytic geometry that are frequently encountered in computer graphics. For completeness, I have included a short review of important elements of Euclidean geometry with which you should be familiar. Perhaps the most important topics that you should try to understand concern the definitions of straight lines in space, 3D planes, and how points of intersection are computed. Another useful topic is the role of parameters in describing lines and line segments, and their intersection.

Review of geometry

In the 3rd century BCE Euclid laid the foundations of geometry that have been taught in schools for centuries. In the 19th century, mathematicians such as Bernhard Riemann (1809–1900) and Nicolai Lobachevsky (1793–1856) transformed this traditional Euclidean geometry with ideas such as curved space and spaces with higher dimensions. Although none of these developments affect computer graphics, they do place Euclid's theorems in a specific context: a set of axioms that apply to flat surfaces. We have probably all been taught that parallel lines don't meet, and that the internal angles of a triangle sum to 180°, but these things are only true in specific situations. As soon as the surface or space becomes curved, such rules break down. So let's review some rules and observations that apply to shapes drawn on a flat surface.

Angles

By definition, 360° or 2π [radians] measure one revolution. The reader should be familiar with both units of measurement, and how to convert from one to the other (see page 26). Figure 10.1 shows examples of *adjacent/ supplementary* angles (sum to 180°) *opposite* angles (equal), and *complementary* angles (sum to 90°).

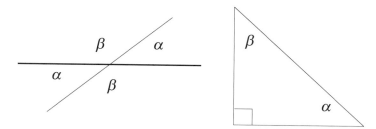

Figure 10.1 *Examples of adjacent/supplementary, opposite and complementary angles.*

Intercept theorems

Figures 10.2 and 10.3 show scenarios involving intersecting lines and parallel lines that give rise to the following observations:

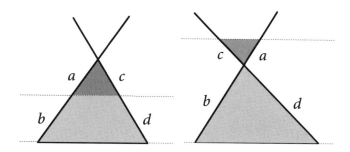

Figure 10.2 *1st intercept theorem.*

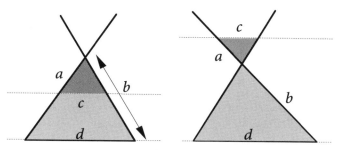

Figure 10.3 *2nd intercept theorem.*

- First intercept theorem:

$$\frac{a+b}{a} = \frac{c+d}{c}, \qquad \frac{b}{a} = \frac{d}{c} \qquad (10.1)$$

- Second intercept theorem:

$$\frac{a}{b} = \frac{c}{d} \qquad (10.2)$$

Golden section

The *golden section* is widely used in art and architecture to represent an 'ideal' ratio for the height and width of an object. Its origins stem from the interaction between a circle and triangle and give rise to the following relationship:

$$b = \frac{a}{2}\left(\sqrt{5}-1\right) \approx 0.618a \qquad (10.3)$$

The rectangle in Figure 10.4 has the proportions

height = 0.618 × *width.*

However, it is interesting to note that the most widely observed rectangle – the television screen – bears no relation to this ratio.

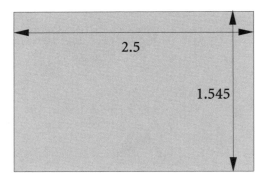

2.5

1.545

Figure 10.4 A rectangle with a height to width ratio equal to the Golden Section.

Triangles

The rules associated with *interior* and *exterior* angles of a triangle are very useful in solving all sorts of geometric problems. Figure 10.5 shows two diagrams identifying interior and exterior angles. We can see that the sum of the interior angles is 180°, and that the exterior angles of a triangle are equal to the sum of the opposite angles:

$$\alpha + \beta + \theta = 180°$$ (10.4)

$$\alpha' = \theta + \beta$$ (10.5)

$$\beta' = \alpha + \theta$$ (10.6)

$$\theta' = \alpha + \beta$$ (10.7)

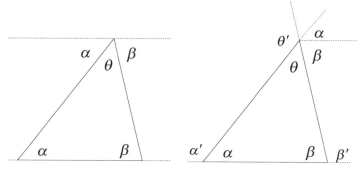

Figure 10.5 *Relationship between interior and exterior angles.*

Centre of gravity of a triangle

A *median* is a straight line joining a vertex of a triangle to the mid-point of the opposite side. When all three medians are drawn, they intersect at a common point, which is also the triangle's *centre of gravity*. The centre of gravity divides all the medians in the ratio 2 : 1. Figure 10.6 illustrates this arrangement.

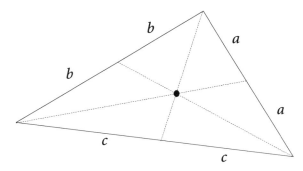

Figure 10.6 *The three medians of a triangle intersect as its centre of gravity.*

Isosceles triangle

Figure 10.7 shows an *isosceles* triangle, which has two equal sides of length l and equal base angles α. The triangle's altitude and area are

$$h = \sqrt{l^2 - \left(\frac{c}{2}\right)^2} \quad A = \frac{1}{2}c \cdot h \quad\quad (10.8)$$

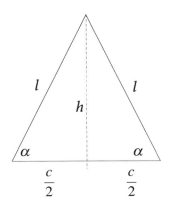

Figure 10.7 *An isosceles triangle has two equal sides l and equal base angles α.*

Equilateral triangle

An *equilateral* triangle has three equal sides of length l and equal angles of 60°. The triangle's altitude and area are

$$h = \frac{\sqrt{3}}{2}l \qquad A = \frac{\sqrt{3}}{4}l^2 \tag{10.9}$$

Right triangle

Figure 10.8 shows a *right* triangle with its obligatory right angle. The triangle's altitude and area are

$$h = \frac{ab}{c} \quad A = \frac{1}{2}ab \tag{10.10}$$

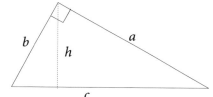

Figure 10.8 *A Right angled triangle.*

Theorem of Thales

Figure 10.9 illustrates the theorem of Thales, which states that the right angle of a right triangle lies on the circumcircle over the hypotenuse.

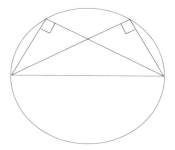

Figure 10.9 *The Theorem of Thales states that the right angle of a right triangle lies on the circumcircle over the hypotenuse.*

Theorem of Pythagoras

Despite its name, there is substantial evidence to show that this theorem was known by the Babylonians a millennium before Pythagoras. However, he is credited with its proof. Figure 10.10 illustrates the well-known relationship

$$c^2 = a^2 + b^2 \qquad (10.11)$$

from which one can show that

$$\sin^2(\alpha) + \cos^2(\alpha) = 1 \qquad (10.12)$$

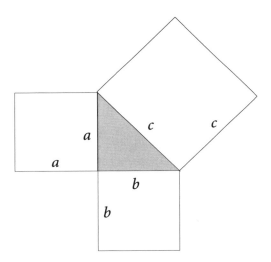

Figure 10.10 *The Theorem of Pythagoras states that*
$$c^2 = a^2 + b^2$$

Quadrilaterals

Quadrilaterals have four sides. Examples include the square, rectangle, trapezoid, parallelogram and rhombus, whose interior angles sum to 360°. As the square and rectangle are such familiar shapes, we will only consider the other three.

Trapezoid

Figure 10.11 shows a *trapezoid* which has one pair of parallel sides h apart. The mid-line m and area are given by

$$m = \tfrac{1}{2}(a + b) \quad A = m \cdot h \tag{10.13}$$

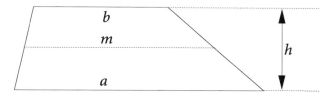

Figure 10.11 *A trapezoid with one pair of parallel sides.*

Parallelogram

Figure 10.12 shows a *parallelogram*. This is formed from two pairs of intersecting parallel lines, so it has equal opposite sides and equal opposite angles. The altitude and diagonal lengths are given by

$$h = b \cdot \sin\alpha \tag{10.14}$$

$$d_{1,2} = \sqrt{a^2 + b^2 \pm 2a\sqrt{b^2 - h^2}} \tag{10.15}$$

and the area by

$$A = a \cdot h \tag{10.16}$$

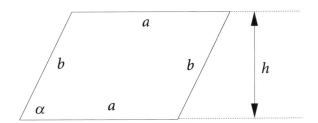

Figure 10.12 *A parallelogram formed by two pairs of parallel lines.*

Rhombus

Figure 10.13 shows a *rhombus*, which is a parallelogram with four sides of equal length *a*. The area is given by

$$A = a^2 \cdot \sin(\alpha) = \frac{d_1 d_2}{2} \qquad (10.17)$$

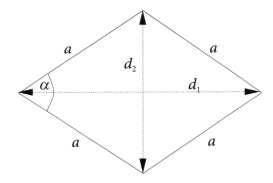

Figure 10.13 *A rhombus is a parallelogram with four equal sides.*

Regular polygon (*n*-gon)

Figure 10.14 shows part of a regular *n*-gon with outer radius R_o, inner radius R_i and edge length a_n. Table 10.1 shows the relationship between the area, *an*, R_i and R_o for different polygons.

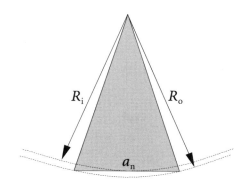

Figure 10.14 *Part of a regular gon showing the internal and outer radii and the edge length.*

Table 10.1 The area A_n, edge length a_n, internal radius R_i and external radius R_o for different polygons

n	$a_n = 2R_i \tan(180°/n)$	$R_i = R_o \cos(180°/n)$	$R_o^2 = R_i^2 + \dfrac{1}{4}a_n^2$
n	$A_n = \dfrac{n}{4}a_n^2 \cot(180°/n)$	$A_n = \dfrac{n}{2}R_0^2 \sin(360°/n)$	$A_n = nR_i^2 \tan(180°/n)$
5	$a_5 = 2R_i \sqrt{5 - 2\sqrt{5}}$	$R_i = \dfrac{R_o}{4}\left(\sqrt{5}+1\right)$	$R_o = R_i\left(\sqrt{5}-1\right)$
5	$A_5 = \dfrac{a_5^2}{4}\sqrt{25 + 10\sqrt{5}}$	$A_5 = \dfrac{5}{8}R_o^2\sqrt{10 + 2\sqrt{5}}$	$A_5 = 5R_i^2\sqrt{5 - 2\sqrt{5}}$
6	$a_6 = \dfrac{2}{3}R_i\sqrt{3}$	$R_i = \dfrac{R_o}{2}\sqrt{3}$	$R_o = \dfrac{2}{3}R_i\sqrt{3}$
6	$A_6 = \dfrac{3}{2}a_6^2\sqrt{3}$	$A_6 = \dfrac{3}{2}R_o^2\sqrt{3}$	$A_6 = 2R_i^2\sqrt{3}$
8	$a_8 = 2R_i\left(\sqrt{2}-1\right)$	$R_i = \dfrac{R_o}{2}\sqrt{2 + \sqrt{2}}$	$R_o = R_i\sqrt{4 - 2\sqrt{2}}$
8	$A_8 = 2a_8^2\left(\sqrt{2}+1\right)$	$A_8 = 2R_o^2\sqrt{2}$	$A_8 = 8R_i^2\left(\sqrt{2}-1\right)$
10	$a_{10} = \dfrac{2}{5}R_i\sqrt{25 - 10\sqrt{5}}$	$R_i = \dfrac{R_c}{4}\sqrt{10 + 2\sqrt{5}}$	$R_o = \dfrac{R_i}{5}\sqrt{50 - 10\sqrt{5}}$
10	$A_{10} = \dfrac{5}{2}a_{10}^2\sqrt{5 + 2\sqrt{5}}$	$A_{10} = \dfrac{5}{4}R_o^2\sqrt{10 - 2\sqrt{5}}$	$A_{10} = 2R_i^2\sqrt{25 - 10\sqrt{5}}$

Circle

The circumference and area of a *circle* are given by

$$C = \pi \cdot d = 2\pi \cdot r \tag{10.18}$$

$$A = \pi \cdot r^2 = \pi \frac{d^2}{4} \tag{10.19}$$

where $d = 2r$.

An *annulus* is the area between two concentric circles, as shown in Figure 10.15, and its area is given by

$$A = \pi(R^2 - r^2) = \frac{\pi}{4}(D^2 - d^2) \tag{10.20}$$

where $D = 2R$ and $d = 2r$.

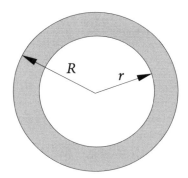

***Figure 10.15** An annulus formed from two concentric circles.*

Figure 10.16 shows a *sector* of a circle, whose area is given by

$$A = \frac{\alpha}{360°} \pi \cdot r^2 \tag{10.21}$$

Figure 10.17 shows a *segment* of a circle, whose area is given by

$$A = \frac{r^2}{2}(\alpha - \sin(\alpha)) \quad (\alpha \text{ is in radians}) \tag{10.22}$$

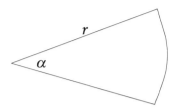

Figure 10.16 A sector of a circle defined by the angle α.

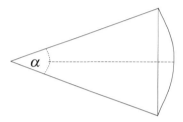

Figure 10.17 A segment of a circle defined by the angle α.

The area of an *ellipse* with major and minor radii *a* and *b* is given by

$$A = \pi \cdot a \cdot b \tag{10.23}$$

2D analytical geometry

In this section we briefly examine familiar descriptions of geometric elements and ways of computing intersections.

Equation of a straight line

The well-known equation of a line is

$$y = mx + c \tag{10.24}$$

where m is the slope and c the intersection with the y-axis, as shown in Figure 10.18. This is called the *normal form*.

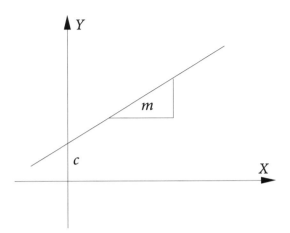

Figure 10.18 *The normal form of the straight line is*
$y = mx + c.$

Given two points (x_1, y_1) and (x_2, y_2) we can state

$$\frac{y - y_1}{x - x_1} = \frac{y_2 - y_1}{x_2 - x_1} \qquad (10.25)$$

which yields

$$y = (x - x_1)\frac{y_2 - y_1}{x_2 - x_1} + y_1 \qquad (10.26)$$

Although these equations have their uses, the more general form is much more convenient:

$$ax + by + c = 0 \qquad (10.27)$$

As we shall see, this equation possesses some interesting qualities.

The Hessian normal form

Figure 10.19 shows a line whose orientation is controlled by a normal unit vector $\mathbf{n} = [a \ b]^T$. If $P(x, y)$ is any point on the line, then $\mathbf{p}$ is a position vector where $\mathbf{p} = [x \ y]^T$ and d is the perpendicular distance from the origin to the line.

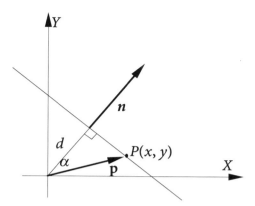

Figure 10.19 *The orientation of a line can be controlled by a normal vector **n** and distance **d**.*

Therefore $\dfrac{d}{|\mathbf{p}|} = \cos(\alpha)$

and

$$d = |\mathbf{p}|\cos(\alpha) \tag{10.28}$$

But the dot product $\mathbf{n} \cdot \mathbf{p}$ is given by

$$\mathbf{n} \cdot \mathbf{p} = |\mathbf{n}||\mathbf{p}|\cos(\alpha) = ax + by \tag{10.29}$$

which implies that

$$ax + by = d|\mathbf{n}| \tag{10.30}$$

and because $|\mathbf{n}| = 1$ we can write

$$ax + by - d = 0 \tag{10.31}$$

where (x, y) is a point on the line, a and b are the components of a unit vector normal to the line and d is the perpendicular distance from the origin to the line. The distance d is positive when the normal vector points away from the origin, otherwise it is negative.

Let's consider two examples.

- *Example 1.* Find the equation of a line whose normal vector is $[3\ 4]^{\mathrm{T}}$ and the perpendicular distance from the origin to the line is 1.

To begin, we normalize the normal vector to its unit form.

Therefore if $\mathbf{n} = [3\ 4]^{\mathrm{T}}$, $|\mathbf{n}| = \sqrt{3^2 + 4^2} = 5$

The equation of the line is

$$\frac{3}{5}x + \frac{4}{5}y - 1 = 0$$

- *Example 2.* Given $y = 2x + 1$, what is the Hessian normal form?

Rearranging the equation, we get

$$2x - y + 1 = 0$$

If we want the normal vector to point away from the origin we multiply by -1:

$$-2x + y - 1 = 0$$

Normalize the normal vector to a unit form, i.e.

$$(\text{i.e. } \sqrt{(-2)^2 + 1^2} = \sqrt{5}$$

$$-\frac{2}{\sqrt{5}}x + \frac{1}{\sqrt{5}}y - \frac{1}{\sqrt{5}} = 0$$

Therefore, the perpendicular distance from the origin to the line and the unit normal vector are respectively

$$\frac{1}{\sqrt{5}} \quad \text{and} \quad \left[\frac{-2}{\sqrt{5}}\ \frac{1}{\sqrt{5}}\right]^{\mathrm{T}}$$

The two signs from the square root provide the alternate directions of the vector, and the sign of d.

As the Hessian normal form involves a unit normal vector, we can incorporate the vector's direction cosines within the equation:

$$x \cos(\alpha) + y \sin(\alpha) - d = 0 \tag{10.32}$$

where α is the angle between the perpendicular and the x-axis.

Space partitioning

The Hessian normal form provides a very useful way of partitioning space into two zones: points above the line in the partition that includes the normal vector, and points in the opposite partition. This is illustrated in Figure 10.20.

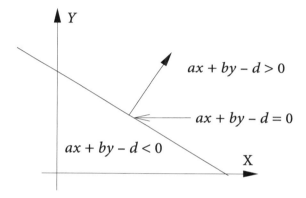

Figure 10.20 *The Hessian normal form of the line equation partitions space into two zones.*

Given the equation

$$ax + by - d = 0 \tag{10.33}$$

a point (x, y) on the line satisfies the equation. But if we substitute another point (x_1, y_1) which is in the partition in the direction of the normal vector, it creates the inequality

$$ax_1 + by_1 - d > 0 \tag{10.34}$$

Conversely, a point (x_2, y_2) which is in the partition opposite to the direction of the normal vector creates the inequality

$$ax_2 + by_2 - d < 0 \tag{10.35}$$

This space-partitioning feature of the Hessian normal form is useful in clipping lines against polygonal windows.

The Hessian normal form from two points

Given two points (x_1, y_1) and (x_2, y_2), we can compute the values of a, b and d for the Hessian normal form as follows. To begin with, we observe:

$$\frac{y - y_1}{x - x_1} = \frac{y_2 - y_1}{x_2 - x_1} = \frac{\Delta y}{\Delta x} \tag{10.36}$$

therefore $(y - y_1)\Delta x = (x - x_1)\Delta y$ (10.37)

and $x\Delta y - y\Delta x - x_1\Delta y + y_1\Delta x = 0$ (10.38)

which is the general equation of a straight line. For the Hessian normal form,

$$\sqrt{\Delta x^2 + \Delta y^2} = 1$$

Therefore, the Hessian normal form is given by

$$\frac{x\Delta y - y\Delta x - (x_1\Delta y - y_1\Delta x)}{\sqrt{\Delta x^2 + \Delta y^2}} = 0 \tag{10.39}$$

Let's test this with an example. Given the following points: $(x_1, y_1) = (0, 1)$ and $(x_2, y_2) = (1, 0)$; $\Delta x = 1, \Delta y = -1$.

Therefore, using (10.38),

$$x(-1) - y(1) - (0 \times -1 - 1 \times 1) = 0$$

$$- x - y + 1 = 0 \tag{10.40}$$

which is the general equation for the line. We now convert it to the Hessian normal form:

$$\frac{-x - y + 1}{\sqrt{1^2 + (-1)^2}} = \frac{-x - y + 1}{\sqrt{2}} = 0$$

$$-\frac{x}{\sqrt{2}} - \frac{y}{\sqrt{2}} + \frac{1}{\sqrt{2}} = 0 \tag{10.41}$$

The choice of sign in the denominator anticipates the two directions for the normal vector, and the sign of d.

Intersection points

Intersection point of two straight lines

Given two line equations of the form

$$a_1x + b_1y + c_1 = 0$$

$$a_2x + b_2y + c_2 = 0 \qquad (10.42)$$

the intersection point (x_i, y_i) is given by

$$x_i = \frac{b_1c_2 - b_2c_1}{a_1b_2 - a_2b_1} \quad \text{and} \quad y_i = \frac{c_1a_2 - c_2a_1}{a_1b_2 - a_2b_1} \qquad (10.43)$$

If the denominator is zero, the equations are linearly dependent, indicating that there is no intersection.

Intersection point of two line segments

We are often concerned with line segments in computer graphics as they represent the edges of shapes and objects. So let's investigate how to compute the intersection of two 2D-line segments.

Figure 10.21 shows two line segments defined by their endpoints $(P_1 - P_2)$ and $(P_3 - P_4)$. If we locate position vectors at these points, we can write the following vector equations to identify the point of intersection:

$$\mathbf{P}_i = \mathbf{P}_1 + t(\mathbf{P}_2 - \mathbf{P}_1)$$

$$\mathbf{P}_i = \mathbf{P}_3 + s(\mathbf{P}_4 - \mathbf{P}_3) \qquad (10.44)$$

where parameters s and t vary between 0 and 1. For the point of intersection, we can write

$$\mathbf{P}_1 + t(\mathbf{P}_2 - \mathbf{P}_1) = \mathbf{P}_3 + s(\mathbf{P}_4 - \mathbf{P}_3) \qquad (10.45)$$

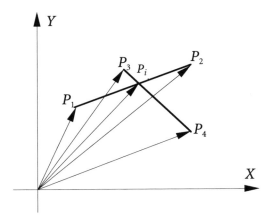

Figure 10.21 *Two line segments with their associated position vectors.*

Therefore, the parameters s and t are given by

$$s = \frac{(\mathbf{P}_1 - \mathbf{P}_3) + t(\mathbf{P}_2 - \mathbf{P}_1)}{(\mathbf{P}_4 - \mathbf{P}_3)}$$

$$t = \frac{(\mathbf{P}_3 - \mathbf{P}_1) + s(\mathbf{P}_4 - \mathbf{P}_3)}{(\mathbf{P}_2 - \mathbf{P}_1)} \qquad (10.46)$$

From (10.46) we can write

$$t = \frac{(x_3 - x_1) + s(x_4 - x_3)}{(x_2 - x_1)}$$

$$t = \frac{(y_3 - y_1) + s(y_4 - y_3)}{(y_2 - y_1)} \qquad (10.47)$$

which yields

$$t = \frac{x_1(y_4 - y_3) + x_3(y_1 - y_4) + x_4(y_3 - y_1)}{(y_2 - y_1)(x_4 - x_3) - (x_2 - x_1)(y_4 - y_3)}$$

and similarly,

$$s = \frac{x_1(y_3 - y_2) + x_2(y_3 - y_2) + x_3(y_2 - y_1)}{(y_4 - y_1)(x_2 - x_1) - (x_4 - x_3)(y_2 - y_1)} \qquad (10.48)$$

Let's test (10.48) with two examples to illustrate how this equation can be used in practice. The first example will demonstrate an intersection condition, and the second demonstrates a touching condition.

- *Example 1.* Figure 10.22a shows two line segments intersecting, with an obvious intersection point of (1.5, 0.0). The coordinates of the line segments are

$$(x_1, y_1) = (1, 0) \qquad (x_2, y_2) = (2, 0)$$
$$(x_3, y_3) = (1.5, -1.0) \quad (x_4, y_4) = (1.5, 1.0)$$

therefore

$$t = \frac{1(1-(-1)) + 1.5(0-1) + 1.5(-1-0)}{(0-0)(1.5\text{-}1.5) - (2-1)(1-(-1))}$$

$$t = \frac{2 - 1.5 - 1.5}{-2} = 0.5$$

and

$$s = \frac{1(-1-0) + 2(0-(-1)) + 1.5(0-0)}{(1-(-1))(2-1) - (1.5 - 1.5)(0-0)} = 0.5$$

Substituting t and s in (10.44) we get $(x_i, y_i) = (1.5, 0.0)$, as predicted.

- *Example 2.* Figure 10.22b shows two line segments touching at $(1.5, 0.0)$. The coordinates of the line segments are

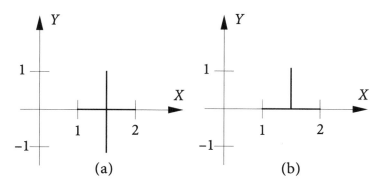

(a) (b)

Figure 10.22 (a) Shows two line segments intersecting, and (b) shows two line segments touching.

$$(x_1, y_1) = (1, 0) \qquad (x_2, y_2) = (2, 0)$$

$$(x_3, y_3) = (1.5, 0.0) \qquad (x_4, y_4) = (1.5, 1.0)$$

therefore

$$t = \frac{1(1.0-0.0) + 1.5(0.0-1.0) + 1.5(0.0-0.0)}{(0.0-0.0)(1.5-1.5) - (2.0-1.0)(1.0-0.0)}$$

$$t = \frac{1.0-1.5}{-1.0} = 0.5$$

$$s = \frac{1(0-0) + 2(0-0) + 1.5(0-0)}{(1-0)(2-1) - (1.5-1.5)(0-0)}$$

$$s = \frac{0}{1} = 0$$

The zero value of s confirms that the lines touch, rather than intersect, and $t = 0.5$ confirms that the touching takes place halfway along the line segment.

Point inside a triangle

We often require to test whether a point is inside, outside or touching a triangle. Let's examine two ways of performing this operation. The first is related to finding the area of a triangle.

Area of a triangle

Let's declare a triangle formed by the anti-clockwise points $(x_1, y_1), (x_2, y_2)$ and (x_3, y_3), as shown in Figure 10.23. The area of the triangle is given by:

$$A = (x_2 - x_1)(y_3 - y_1) - \tfrac{1}{2}(x_2 - x_1)(y_2 - y_1) - \tfrac{1}{2}(x_2 - x_3)(y_3 - y_2)$$
$$- \tfrac{1}{2}(x_3 - x_1)(y_3 - y_1)$$

which simplifies to

$$A = \tfrac{1}{2}[x_1(y_2 - y_3) + x_2(y_3 - y_1) + x_3(y_1 - y_2)]$$

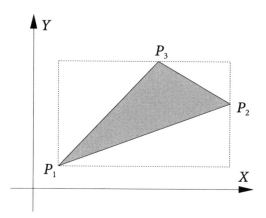

Figure 10.23 *The area of the triangle is computed by subtracting the smaller triangles from the rectangular area.*

and this can be further simplified to

$$A = \frac{1}{2} \begin{vmatrix} x_1 & y_1 & 1 \\ x_2 & y_2 & 1 \\ x_3 & y_3 & 1 \end{vmatrix} \quad\quad (10.49)$$

Figure 10.24 shows two triangles with opposing vertex sequences. If we calculate the area of the top triangle with anti-clockwise vertices, we obtain

$$A = \tfrac{1}{2}[1(2-4) + 3(4-2) + 2(2-2)] = 2$$

whereas the area of the bottom triangle with clockwise vertices is

$$A = \tfrac{1}{2}[1(2-0) + 3(0-2) + 2(2-2)] = -2$$

So the technique is sensitive to vertex direction. We can exploit this sensitivity to test if a point is inside or outside a triangle.

Consider the scenario shown in Figure 10.25, where the point P_t is inside the triangle (P_1, P_2, P_3).

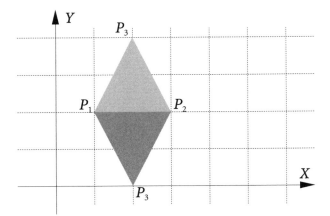

Figure 10.24 *The top triangle has anti-clockwise vertices, and the bottom triangle clockwise vertices.*

- If the area of triangle (P_1, P_2, P_t) is positive, P_t must be to the left of the line (P_1, P_2).
- If the area of triangle (P_2, P_3, P_t) is positive, P_t must be to the left of the line (P_2, P_3).
- If the area of triangle (P_3, P_1, P_t) is positive, P_t must be to the left of the line (P_3, P_1).

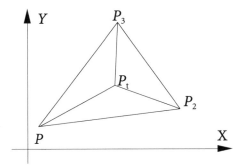

Figure 10.25 *If the point P_t is inside the triangle, it is always to the left as the boundary is traversed in an anti-clockwise sequence.*

If all the above tests are positive, P_t is inside the triangle. Furthermore, if one area is zero and the other areas are positive, the point is on the boundary, and if two areas are zero and the other positive, the point is on a vertex.

Let's now investigate how the Hessian normal form provides a similar function.

Hessian normal form

We can determine whether a point is inside, touching or outside a triangle by representing the triangle's edges in the Hessian normal form, and testing which partition the point is located in. If we arrange that the normal vectors are pointing towards the inside of the triangle, any point inside the triangle will create a positive result when tested against the edge equation. In the following calculations there is no need to ensure that the normal vector is a unit vector.

To illustrate this in action, consider the scenario shown in Figure 10.26 where we see a triangle formed by the points $(1, 1), (3, 1)$ and $(2, 3)$. With reference to (10.38) we compute the three line equations:

1 The line between $(1, 1)$ and $(3, 1)$:

$$0(x - 1) + 2(1 - y) = 0$$

$$-2y + 2 = 0 \qquad (10.50)$$

Multiply (10.50) by -1 to reverse the normal vector:

$$2y - 2 = 0 \qquad (10.51)$$

2 The line between $(3, 1)$ and $(2, 3)$:

$$2(x - 3) + (-1)(1 - y) = 0$$

$$2x - 6 - 1 + y = 0$$

$$2x + y - 7 = 0 \qquad (10.52)$$

Multiply (10.52) by -1 to reverse the normal vector:

$$-2x - y + 7 = 0 \qquad (10.53)$$

3 The line between $(2, 3)$ and $(1, 1)$:

$$(-2)(x - 2) + (-1)(3 - y) = 0$$

$$-2x + 4 - 3 + y = 0$$

$$-2x + y + 1 = 0 \tag{10.54}$$

Multiply (10.54) by -1 to reverse the normal vector:

$$2x - y - 1 = 0$$

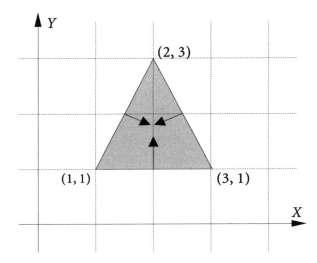

Figure 10.26 *The triangle is formed from three line equations expressed in the Hessian normal form. Any point inside the triangle can be found by evaluating the equations.*

Thus the three line equations for the triangle are

$$2y - 2 = 0$$

$$-2x - y + 7 = 0$$

$$2x - y - 1 = 0 \tag{10.55}$$

We are only interested in the sign of the left-hand expressions:

$$2y - 2$$

$$-2x - y + 7$$

$$2x - y - 1 \tag{10.56}$$

which can be tested for any arbitrary point (x, y). If they are all positive, the point is inside the triangle. If one expression is negative, the point is outside. If one expression is zero, the point is on an edge, and if two expressions are zero, the point is on a vertex.

Just as a quick test, consider the point $(2, 2)$. The three expressions (10.56) are positive, which confirms that the point is inside the triangle. The point $(3, 3)$ is obviously outside the triangle, which is confirmed by two positive results and one negative. Finally, the point $(2, 3)$, which is a vertex, gives one positive result and two zero results.

Intersection of a circle with a straight line

The equation of a circle has already been given in the previous chapter, so we will now consider how to compute its intersection with a straight line.

We begin by testing the equation of a circle with the normal form of the line equation:

$$x^2 + y^2 = r^2 \text{ and } y = mx + c$$

By substituting the line equation in the circle's equation we discover the two intersection points:

$$x_{1,2} = \frac{-mc \pm \sqrt{r^2(1+m^2)-c^2}}{1+m^2}$$

$$y_{1,2} = \frac{c \pm m\sqrt{r^2(1+m^2)-c^2}}{1+m^2} \tag{10.57}$$

Let's test this result with the scenario shown in Figure 10.27. Using the normal form of the line equation, we have

$$y = x + 1 \text{ where } m = 1 \text{ and } c = 1$$

Substituting these values in (10.57) yields

$x_{1,2} = -1, 0$ and $y_{1,2} = 0, 1$

The actual points of intersection are $(-1, 0)$ and $(0, 1)$.

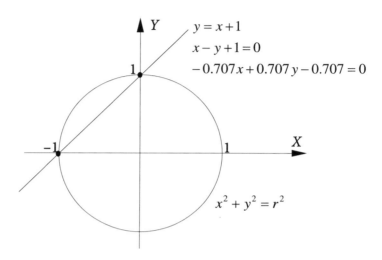

Figure 10.27 *The intersection of a circle with a line defined in its normal form, general form, and the Hessian normal form.*

Testing the equation of the circle with the general equation of the line $ax + by + c = 0$ yields intersections given by

$$x_{1,2} = \frac{-ac \pm b\sqrt{r^2(a^2 + b^2) - c^2}}{a^2 + b^2}$$

$$y_{1,2} = \frac{-bc \pm a\sqrt{r^2(a^2 + b^2) - c^2}}{a^2 + b^2} \qquad (10.58)$$

From Fig. 10.27, the general form of the line equation is

$x - y + 1 = 0$ where $a = 1, b = -1$ and $c = 1$

Substituting these values in (10.58) yields

$x_{1,2} = -1, 0$ and $y_{1,2} = 0, 1$

which gives the same intersection points found above.

Finally, using the Hessian normal form of the line $ax + by - d = 0$ yields intersections given by

$$x_{1,2} = ad \pm b\sqrt{r^2 - d^2}$$

$$y_{1,2} = bd \pm a\sqrt{r^2 - d^2} \tag{10.59}$$

From Fig. 10.27, the Hessian normal form of the line equation is

$$-0.707x + 0.707y - 0.707 = 0$$

where $a = -0.707$, $b = 0.707$ and $d = 0.707$. Substituting these values in (10.59) yields

$$x_{1,2} = -1, 0 \text{ and } y_{1,2} = 0, 1$$

which gives the same intersection points found above. One can readily see the computational benefits of using the Hessian normal form over the other forms of equations.

3D geometry

3D straight lines are best described using vector notation, and it is a good idea to develop strong skills in vector techniques if you wish to solve problems in 3D geometry.

Let's begin this short survey of 3D analytic geometry by describing the equation of a straight line.

Equation of a straight line

We start by using a vector b to define the orientation of the line, and a point a in space through which the vector passes. This scenario is shown in Figure 10.28. Given another point P on the line we can define a vector $t\mathbf{b}$ between a and P, where t is some scalar. The position vector $\mathbf{p}$ is given by

$$\mathbf{p} = \mathbf{a} + t\mathbf{b} \tag{10.60}$$

from which we can obtain the coordinates of the point P:

$$x_p = x_a + tx_b$$
$$y_p = y_a + ty_b$$
$$z_p = z_a + tz_b \qquad\qquad (10.61)$$

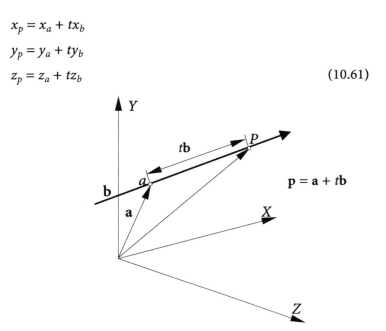

Figure 10.28 *The line equation is based upon the point a and the vector b.*

For example, if $\mathbf{b} = [1\ 2\ 3]^T$ and $a = (2, 3, 4)$, then by setting $t = 1$ we can identify a second point on the line:

$$x_p = 2 + 1 = 3$$
$$y_p = 3 + 2 = 5$$
$$z_p = 4 + 3 = 7$$

In fact, by using different values of t we can slide up and down the line with ease.

If we already have two points in space P_1 and P_2, such as the vertices of an edge, we can represent the line equation using the above vector technique:

$$\mathbf{p} = \mathbf{p}_1 + t(\mathbf{p}_2 - \mathbf{p}_1)$$

where $\mathbf{p}_1$ and $\mathbf{p}_2$ are position vectors to their respective points. Once more, we can write the coordinates of any point P as follows:

$$x_p = x_1 + t(x_2 - x_1)$$
$$y_p = y_1 + t(y_2 - y_1)$$
$$z_p = z_1 + t(z_2 - z_1) \tag{10.62}$$

Point of intersection of two straight lines

Given two straight lines we can test for a point of intersection, but must be prepared for three results:

- a real intersection point
- no intersection point
- an infinite number of intersections (identical lines).

If the line equations are of the form

$$\mathbf{p} = \mathbf{a}_1 + r\mathbf{b}_1$$
$$\mathbf{p} = \mathbf{a}_2 + s\mathbf{b}_2 \tag{10.63}$$

for an intersection we can write

$$\mathbf{a}_1 + r\mathbf{b}_1 = \mathbf{a}_2 + s\mathbf{b}_2 \tag{10.64}$$

which yields

$$x_{a1} + rx_{b1} = x_{a2} + sx_{b2}$$
$$y_{a1} + ry_{b1} = y_{a2} + sy_{b2}$$
$$z_{a1} + rz_{b1} = z_{a2} + sz_{b2} \tag{10.65}$$

We now have three equations in two unknowns, and any value of r and s must hold for all three equations. We begin by selecting two equations that are linearly independent (i.e. one equation is not a scalar multiple of the other) and solve for r and s, which must then satisfy the third equation. If this final substitution fails, then there is no intersection. If all three equations are linearly dependent, they describe two parallel lines, which can never intersect.

To check for linear dependency we rearrange (10.65) as follows:

$$rx_{b1} - sx_{b2} = x_{a2} - x_{a1}$$

$$ry_{b1} - sy_{b2} = y_{a2} - y_{a1}$$

$$rz_{b1} - sz_{b2} = z_{a2} - z_{a1} \tag{10.66}$$

If the determinant Δ of any pair of these equations is zero, then they are dependent. For example, the first two equations of (10.66) form the determinant

$$\Delta = \begin{vmatrix} x_{b1} & -x_{b2} \\ y_{b1} & -y_{b2} \end{vmatrix} \tag{10.67}$$

which, if zero, implies that the two equations can not yield a solution. As it is impossible to predict which pair of equations from (10.66) will be independent, let's express two independent equations as follows:

$$ra_{11} - sa_{12} = b_1$$

$$ra_{21} - sa_{22} = b_2 \tag{10.68}$$

which yields

$$r = \frac{(a_{22}b_1 - a_{12}b_2)}{\Delta} \tag{10.69}$$

$$s = \frac{(a_{21}b_1 - a_{11}b_2)}{\Delta} \tag{10.70}$$

where

$$\Delta = \begin{vmatrix} a_{11} & a_{12} \\ a_{21} & a_{22} \end{vmatrix} \tag{10.71}$$

Solving for r and s we obtain

$$r = \frac{y_{b2}(x_{a2} - x_{a1}) - x_{b2}(y_{a2} - y_{a1})}{x_{b1}y_{b2} - y_{b1}x_{b2}} \tag{10.72}$$

$$s = \frac{y_{b1}(x_{a2} - x_{a1}) - x_{b1}(y_{a2} - y_{a1})}{x_{b1}y_{b2} - y_{b1}x_{b2}} \tag{10.73}$$

As a quick test, consider the intersection of the lines encoded by the following vectors:

$$\mathbf{a}_1 = \begin{bmatrix} 0 \\ 1 \\ 0 \end{bmatrix} \quad \mathbf{b}_1 = \begin{bmatrix} 3 \\ 3 \\ 3 \end{bmatrix} \quad \mathbf{a}_2 = \begin{bmatrix} 0 \\ \frac{1}{2} \\ 0 \end{bmatrix} \quad \mathbf{b}_2 = \begin{bmatrix} 2 \\ 3 \\ 2 \end{bmatrix}$$

Substituting the x and y components in (10.72) and (10.73), we discover

$$r = \tfrac{1}{3} \quad \text{and} \quad s = \tfrac{1}{2}$$

but for these to be consistent, they must satisfy the z component of the original equation:

$$rz_{b1} - sz_{b2} = z_{a2} - z_{a1}$$
$$\tfrac{1}{3} \times 3 - \tfrac{1}{2} \times 2 = 0 - 0$$

which is correct. Therefore, the point of intersection is given by either

$$\mathbf{p}_i = \mathbf{a}_1 + r\mathbf{b}_1 \quad \text{or}$$
$$\mathbf{p}_i = \mathbf{a}_2 + s\mathbf{b}_2$$

Let's try both, just to prove the point:

$$x_i = 0 + \tfrac{1}{3}3 = 1 \qquad x_i = 0 + \tfrac{1}{2}2 = 1$$
$$y_i = 1 + \tfrac{1}{3}3 = 2 \qquad y_i = \tfrac{1}{2} + \tfrac{1}{3}3 = 2$$
$$z_i = 0 + \tfrac{1}{3}3 = 1 \qquad z_i = 0 + \tfrac{1}{2}2 = 1$$

Therefore, the point of intersection point is $(1, 2, 1)$.

Now let's take two lines that don't intersect, and also exhibit some linear dependency:

$$\mathbf{a}_1 = \begin{bmatrix} 0 \\ 1 \\ 0 \end{bmatrix} \quad \mathbf{b}_1 = \begin{bmatrix} 2 \\ 2 \\ 0 \end{bmatrix} \quad \mathbf{a}_2 = \begin{bmatrix} 0 \\ 2 \\ 0 \end{bmatrix} \quad \mathbf{b}_2 = \begin{bmatrix} 2 \\ 2 \\ 1 \end{bmatrix}$$

Taking the x and y components we discover that the determinant Δ is zero, which has identified the linear dependency. Taking the y and z components the determinant is non-zero, which permits us to compute r and s using

$$r = \frac{z_{b2}(y_{a2} - y_{a1}) - y_{b2}(z_{a2} - z_{a1})}{y_{b1}z_{b2} - z_{b1}y_{b2}} \qquad (10.74)$$

$$s = \frac{z_{b1}(y_{a2} - y_{a1}) - y_{b1}(z_{a2} - z_{a1})}{y_{b1}z_{b2} - z_{b1}y_{b2}} \qquad (10.75)$$

$$r = \frac{1(2-1) - 2(0-0)}{2 \times 1 - 0 \times 2} = \frac{1}{2}$$

$$s = \frac{0(2-1) - 2(0-0)}{2 \times 1 - 0 \times 2} = \frac{0}{2} = 0$$

But these values of r and s must also apply to the x components:

$$rx_{b1} - sx_{b2} = x_{a2} - x_{a1}$$

$$\tfrac{1}{2} \times 2 - 0 \times 2 \neq 0 - 0$$

which they clearly do not, therefore the lines do not intersect.

Now let's proceed with the equation of a plane, and then look at how to compute the intersection of a line with a plane using a similar technique.

Equation of a plane

The Hessian normal form for a plane is just an extension of the 2D equation for a line. Figure 10.29 illustrates the scenario where we see a plane's orientation determined by a unit surface normal **n**. The distance d is the perpendicular distance from the origin to the plane.

We can write

$$\frac{d}{|\mathbf{p}|} = \cos(\alpha)$$

and

$$d = |\mathbf{p}|\cos(\alpha) \qquad (10.76)$$

But the dot product $\mathbf{n} \cdot \mathbf{p}$ is given by

$$\mathbf{n} \cdot \mathbf{p} = |\mathbf{n}||\mathbf{p}|\cos(\alpha) = ax + by + cz \qquad (10.77)$$

which implies that

$$ax + by + cz = d|\mathbf{n}| \tag{10.78}$$

and because $|\mathbf{n}| = 1$ we can write

$$ax + by + cz - d = 0 \tag{10.79}$$

where (x, y, z) is a point on the plane; a, b, c are the components of a unit vector normal to the plane; and d is the perpendicular distance from the origin to the plane.

Let's now consider an example. Once more, if the normal vector points away from the origin, d is positive, otherwise it is negative.

Find the equation of a plane whose normal vector is $[1\,2\,2]^T$ and the perpendicular distance from the origin to the plane is 1.

To begin, we normalize the normal vector to its unit form. Therefore, if $\mathbf{n} = [1\,2\,2]^T$, $|\mathbf{n}| = \sqrt{1^2 + 2^2 + 2^2} = 3$ and the plane equation is

$$\frac{1}{3}x + \frac{2}{3}y + \frac{2}{3}z - 1 = 0$$

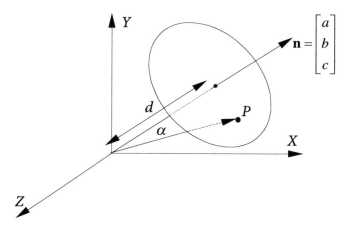

Figure 10.29 *The Hessian normal form for a plane employs the dot product of the normal vector and the position vector to any point to create the place equation.*

Space partitioning

The Hessian normal form for a 2D line exhibited a space partitioning effect, which is continued with a 3D plane. When we compute the expression $ax + by + cz - d$, points in the space partition containing the normal vector will create a positive value, whereas points in the opposite partition yield a negative value. In the above example, for instance, the point $(30, 30, 30)$ is clearly in the partition away from the origin and yields a value of $+49$, whereas the point $(0, \frac{1}{2}, \frac{1}{2})$ is in the partition containing the origin and yields a value of $-\frac{1}{3}$. Thus we can easily test to see which side a point is relative to a plane.

Point of intersection of a line and a plane

Now that we have a vector definition of a line and a plane, it should be relatively easy to see if and where they intersect. Figure 10.30 shows the scenario where a plane is defined by its unit normal vector **n** and distance to the origin d. The line is defined by a point E, position vector **e**, and direction vector **f**. The point of intersection is defined as P and position vector **p**.

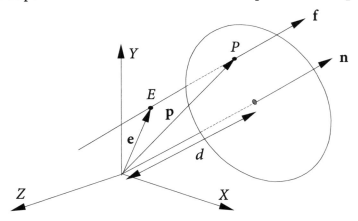

Figure 10.30 *The vectors used to define a line, plane and the point of intersection P.*

If P is the point of intersection, we can write

$$\mathbf{p} = \mathbf{e} + t\mathbf{f} \text{ where } t \text{ is a scalar} \qquad (10.80)$$

We can also write the plane equation as

$$\mathbf{n} \cdot \mathbf{p} = d \qquad (10.81)$$

Substituting (10.81) in (10.80) we get

$$\mathbf{n} \cdot (\mathbf{e} + t\mathbf{f}) = d \qquad (10.82)$$

which yields

$$t = \frac{d - \mathbf{n} \cdot \mathbf{e}}{\mathbf{n} \cdot \mathbf{f}} \qquad (10.83)$$

If the vectors are declared as follows:

$$\mathbf{n} = \begin{bmatrix} a \\ b \\ c \end{bmatrix} \qquad \mathbf{e} = \begin{bmatrix} x_e \\ y_e \\ z_e \end{bmatrix} \qquad \mathbf{f} = \begin{bmatrix} x_f \\ y_f \\ z_f \end{bmatrix} \qquad (10.84)$$

we can write

$$t = \frac{d - (ax_e + by_e + cz_e)}{ax_f + by_f + cz_f} \qquad (10.85)$$

Given a set of vectors we can compute the value of t and substitute it in (10.80) to obtain the point of intersection.

Let's take a very simple example to see how it works. Figure 10.31 shows a vertical plane parallel with the YZ plane, which intersects with a line in the XY plane, where

$$\mathbf{n} = \begin{bmatrix} 1 \\ 0 \\ 0 \end{bmatrix} \qquad \mathbf{e} = \begin{bmatrix} 0 \\ 1 \\ 0 \end{bmatrix} \qquad \mathbf{f} = \begin{bmatrix} 1 \\ 1 \\ 0 \end{bmatrix} \qquad d = 2$$

Using (10.85),

$$t = \frac{2 - (1 \times 0 + 0 \times 1 + 0 \times 0)}{1 \times 1 + 0 \times 1 + 0 \times 0} = \frac{2}{1} = 2$$

$x_i = 0 + 2 \times 1 = 2$

$y_i = 1 + 2 \times 1 = 3$

$z_1 = 0 + 2 \times 0 = 0$

Therefore the point of intersection is $(2, 3, 0)$, as confirmed by Figure 10.31.

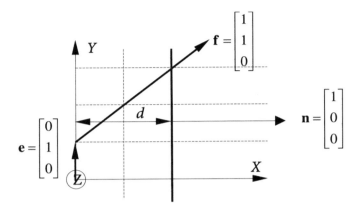

Figure 10.30 *The vectors used to define a line, plane and the point of intersection P.*

But what about non-intersection? Well, this is detected by the condition $n \cdot f = 0$, which is the denominator of (10.85). Thus before computing t, we have to test the denominator for a zero condition.

Point of intersection of a line segment and a plane

In computer graphics we also need to know when an edge intersects a plane surface. To do this, we exploit the same plane equation as above, but express the line segment as a vector equation.

If the line segment has end-points P_1 and P_2, the associated vector is

$$p = p_1 + t(p_2 - p_1) \tag{10.86}$$

where p_1 and p_2 are position vectors to the points. If (10.86) is substituted in (10.81) we get

$$n \cdot (p_1 + t(p_2 - p_1)) = d \tag{10.87}$$

$$t = \frac{d - \mathbf{n} \cdot \mathbf{p}}{\mathbf{n} \cdot (\mathbf{p}_2 - \mathbf{p}_1)} \tag{10.88}$$

$$t = \frac{d - (a \cdot x_{p1} + b \cdot y_{p1} + c \cdot z_{p1})}{a(x_{p2} - x_{p1}) + b(y_{p2} - y_{p1}) + c(z_{p2} - z_{p1})}$$

For the edge to intersect the plane, t must be in the range 0 to 1. The denominator must also be tested for a zero condition to identify an impossible non-intersection.

Summary

Mixing vectors with geometry is a powerful analytical tool, and helps us to solve many problems associated with computer graphics, such as rendering, modelling, collision detection and physically based animation. Unfortunately, there has not been space to investigate every topic, but I hope that what has been covered here will enable you to solve other problems with greater confidence.

Chapter 11

Conclusion

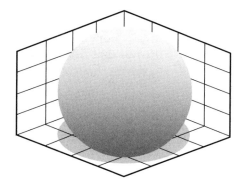

In the previous 10 chapters I have attempted to introduce you to some of the important elements of mathematics employed in computer graphics. I knew from the start that this would be a challenge for two reasons: one was knowing where to start, and the other was knowing where to stop. I assumed that most readers would already be interested in computer animation, games, virtual reality, and so on, and knew something about mathematics. So perhaps the chapters on numbers, algebra and trigonometry provided a common starting point.

The chapters on Cartesian coordinates, vectors, transforms, interpolation, curves and patches are the real core of the book, but while revealing these subjects I was always wondering when to stop. On the one hand, I could have frustrated readers by stopping short of describing a subject completely, and on the other hand lost readers by pursuing a subject to a level beyond the book's objective. Hopefully, I have managed to keep the right balance.

For many readers, what I have covered will be sufficient to enable them to design programs and solve a wide range of problems. For others, the book will provide a useful stepping stone to more advanced texts on mathematics. But what I really hope that I have managed to show is that mathematics is not that difficult, especially when it can be applied to an exciting subject such as computer graphics.

References

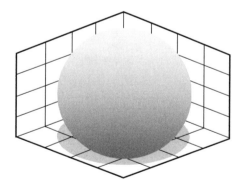

Boyer, C.B. and Merzbach, U.C. (1989) *A History of Mathematics*. Wiley, New York.

Foley et al. (1990) *Computer Graphics: Principles and Practice*.

Glassner et al. (1990) Gems.

Gullberg, J. (1997) *Mathematics: From the Birth of Numbers*. W. W. Norton, New York.

Harris, J.W. and Stocker, H. (1998) *Handbook of Mathematics and Computational Science*. Springer-Verlag, New York.

Index

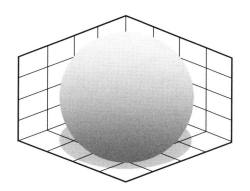

A

algebra · 16
algebraic laws · 17
   associative law · 18
   commutative law · 18
   distributive law · 19
analytic geometry · 181
angles · 182
   adjacent · 182
   complementary · 182
   compound · 30
   exterior · 185
   interior · 185
   measurement · 26
   opposite · 182
   radians · 182
   supplementary · 182
area
   annulus · 192
   circle · 192
   ellipse · 193
   parallelogram · 189
   point inside · 202
   rhombus · 190
   sector · 192
   segment · 192
   trapezoid · 189
Argand, J. · 44
axes
   left-handed · 40
   right-handed · 40

B

Bürgi, J. · 21
Bézier, P. · 152
basis function
   B-spline · 169

Bernstein polynomials · 152
Bernstein, S. · 152

C

Caley, A. · 72
Cartesian *xy*-plane · 34
Chu Shih-chieh · 153
circle · 192
coordinates · 40
   barycentric · 77
   Cartesian · 35
   homogeneous · 75, 77
cosine rule · 29
cross product · *See* vector
   product
curve · 150
   B-spline · 169
   continuity · 170
   cubic B-spline · 168
   Hermite · 172
   non-uniform B-spline · 172
   non-uniform rational B-Spline
      · 173
   quadratic Bézier · 157
   recursive Bézier · 162
   uniform B-spline · 168

D

Descartes, R. · 16, 34
determinant · 62, 122, 212
direction cosines · 100, 103, 196
dot product · 56, 214

E

equation
   circle · 150

cubic · 36
ellipse · 151
linear · 36
linearly dependent · 124
quadratic · 19, 36
straight line · 209
trigonometric · 36
Euclid · 182
Euler angles · 106
Euler rotations · 91
Euler, L. · 10
Euler's rule · 41

F

Fermat, P. · 34

G

Gauss, C. · 73
Gibbs, J. · 44
gimbal lock · 95
Golden section · 184

H

Hamilton, W.R. · 44, 61, 110
Hermite, C. · 140
Hessian normal form · 197, 205

I

indices · 20
intercept theorems · 183
interpolation · 130
    cubic · 135
    linear · 130, 164

non-linear · 133
quaternions · 145
trigonometric · 133
vectors · 141
intersection
    circle with a straight line · 207
    line and a plane · 216
    line segment and a plane · 218
    two line segments · 199
    two straight lines · 199, 211

L

Lambert's law · 58
Liouville, J. · 22
Lobachevsky, N. · 182
logarithms · 21

M

matrix
    Bézier curves · 162
    determinant · 76
    multiplication · 74
    notation · 72
    orthogonal · 106
median · 185
Möbius, A.F. · 77

N

Napier, J. · 21
number line · 10
numbers
    complex · 10
    imaginary · 11
    integers · 9
    irrational · 10

natural · 8
prime · 8
rational · 9
real · 10
transcendental · 22

O

origin · 34

P

parallelogram · 189
    area · 66
Pascal, B. · 34, 153
perspective projection · 126
Pierce, C. and B. · 72
pitch · 92, 106
plane equation · 214
polygon · 37
    area · 38
    back-facing · 59
    planar · 41
polynomial
    Bernstein · 152
    cubic Bernstein · 158
    piecewise · 168

Q

quadrilateral · 188
quaternions · 44, 110
    adding and subtracting ·
        110
    inverse · 111
    matrix · 118
    multiplying · 111
    roll, pitch and yaw · 116

R

radian · 26
rhombus · 190
Riemann, B. · 182
roll · 92, 106

S

scalars · 44
sector · 192
segment · 192
sine rule · 29
space
    camera · 102
    image · 103
    object · 102
    world · 102
space partitioning · 197, 214
straight line equation · 193
    Hessian normal form · 194
    normal form · 193
surface patch · 150
    cubic Bézier · 177
    NURBS · 172–173
    planar · 173
    quadratic Bézier · 174

T

Theorem of Pythagoras · 39, 188
Theorem of Thales · 187
transform
    2D · 70
    2D change of axes · 98
    2D reflection · 71, 80, 87
    2D rotation · 83
    2D scaling · 70, 79, 86

2D shearing · 82
2D translation · 79
3D · 89
3D reflection · 98
3D rotation · 90
3D scaling · 90
3D translation · 89
affine · 86
change of axes · 98
rotating about an axis · 96
transformations · 70
trapezoid · 188
triangle
    area · 202
    center of gravity · 185
    equilateral · 187
    isosceles · 186
    right · 187
trigonometry · 26

V

vector · 44
    addition · 50
    Cartesian · 53
    column · 45, 73
    magnitude · 47
    manipulation · 49
    multiplication · 54
    normalizing · 52
    notation · 45
    position · 51
    product · 60
    right-hand rule · 64
    row · 45
    scalar product · 55
    transforming · 120
    unit · 51
vector product · 19, 55, 60

W

Warren, J. · 44
Wessel, C. · 44

Y

yaw · 92, 106